Shop Management

Frederick Winslow Taylor

Shop Management

The present edition is a reproduction of previous publication of this classic work. Minor typographical errors may have been corrected without note; however, for an authentic reading experience the spelling, punctuation, and capitalization have been retained from the original text.

ISBN: 978-1-64439-568-4

SHOP MANAGEMENT

Through his business in changing the methods of shop management, the writer has been brought into intimate contact over a period of years with the organization of manufacturing and industrial establishments, covering a large variety and range of product, and employing workmen in many of the leading trades.

In taking a broad view of the field of management, the two facts which appear most noteworthy are:

(a) What may be called the great unevenness, or lack of uniformity shown, even in our best run works, in the development of the several elements, which together constitute what is called the management.

(b) The lack of apparent relation between good shop management and the payment of dividends.

Although the day of trusts is here, still practically each of the component companies of the trusts was developed and built up largely through the energies and especial ability of some one or two men who were the master spirits in directing its growth. As a rule, this leader rose from a more or less humble position in one of the departments, say in the commercial or the manufacturing department, until he became the head of his particular section. Having shown especial ability in his line, he was for that reason made manager of the whole establishment.

In examining the organization of works of this class, it will frequently be found that the management of the particular department in which this master spirit has grown up towers to a high point of excellence, his success having been due to a thorough knowledge of all of the smallest requirements of his section, obtained through personal contact, and the gradual training of the men under him to their maximum efficiency.

The remaining departments, in which this man has had but little personal experience, will often present equally glaring examples of inefficiency. And this, mainly because management is not yet looked upon as an art, with laws as exact, and as clearly defined, for instance, as the fundamental principles of engineering, which demand long and careful thought and study. Management is still looked upon as a question of men, the old view being that if you have the right man the methods can be safely left to him.

The following, while rather an extreme case, may still be considered as a fairly typical illustration of the unevenness of management. It became desirable to combine two rival manufactories of chemicals. The great obstacle to this combination, however, and one which for several years had proved insurmountable was that the two men, each of whom occupied the position of owner and manager of his company, thoroughly despised one another. One of these men had risen to the top of his works through the office at the commercial end, and the other had come up from a workman in the factory. Each one was sure that the other was a fool, if not worse. When they were finally combined it was found that each was right in his judgment of the other in a certain way. A comparison of their books showed that the manufacturer was producing his chemicals more than forty per cent cheaper than his rival, while the business man made up the difference by insisting on maintaining the highest quality, and by his superiority in selling, buying, and the management of the commercial side of the business. A combination of the two, however, finally resulted in mutual respect, and saving the forty per cent formerly lost by each man.

The second fact that has struck the writer as most noteworthy is that there is no apparent relation in many, if not most cases, between good shop management and the success or failure of the company, many unsuccessful companies having good shop management while the reverse is true of many which pay large dividends.

We, however, who are primarily interested in the shop, are apt to forget that success, instead of hinging upon shop management, depends in many cases mainly upon other elements, namely,—the location of the company, its financial strength and ability, the efficiency of its business and sales departments, its engineering ability, the superiority of its plant and equipment, or the protection afforded either by patents, combination, location or other partial monopoly.

And even in those cases in which the efficiency of shop management might play an important part it must be remembered that for success no company need be better organized than its competitors.

The most severe trial to which any system can be subjected is that of a business which is in keen competition over a large territory, and in which the labor cost of production forms a large element of the expense, and it is in such establishments that one would naturally expect to find the best type of management.

Yet it is an interesting fact that in several of the largest and most important classes of industries in this country shop practice is still twenty to thirty years behind what might be called modern management. Not only is no attempt made by them to do tonnage or piece work, but the oldest of old-fashioned day work is still in vogue under which one overworked foreman manages the men. The workmen in these shops are still herded in classes, all of those in a class being paid the same wages, regardless of their respective efficiency.

In these industries, however, although they are keenly competitive, the poor type of shop management does not interfere with dividends, since they are in this respect all equally bad.

3

It would appear, therefore, that as an index to the quality of shop management the earning of dividends is but a poor guide.

Any one who has the opportunity and takes the time to study the subject will see that neither good nor bad management is confined to any one system or type. He will find a few instances of good management containing all of the elements necessary for permanent prosperity for both employers and men under ordinary day work, the task system, piece work, contract work, the premium plan, the bonus system and the differential rate; and he will find a very much larger number of instances of bad management under these systems containing as they do the elements which lead to discord and ultimate loss and trouble for both sides.

If neither the prosperity of the company nor any particular type or system furnishes an index to proper management, what then is the touchstone which indicates good or bad management?

The art of management has been defined, "as knowing exactly what you want men to do, and then seeing that they do it in the best and cheapest way."' No concise definition can fully describe an art, but the relations between employers and men form without question the most important part of this art. In considering the subject, therefore, until this part of the problem has been fully discussed, the other phases of the art may be left in the background.

The progress of many types of management is punctuated by a series of disputes, disagreements and compromises between employers and men, and each side spends more than a considerable portion of its time thinking and talking over the injustice which it receives at the hands of the other. All such types are out of the question, and need not be considered.

It is safe to say that no system or scheme of management should be considered which does not in the long run give satisfaction to

4

both employer and employee, which does not make it apparent that their best interests are mutual, and which does not bring about such thorough and hearty cooperation that they can pull together instead of apart. It cannot be said that this condition has as yet been at all generally recognized as the necessary foundation for good management. On the contrary, it is still quite generally regarded as a fact by both sides that in many of the most vital matters the best interests of employers are necessarily opposed to those of the men. In fact, the two elements which we will all agree are most wanted on the one hand by the men and on the other hand by the employers are generally looked upon as antagonistic.

What the workmen want from their employers beyond anything else is high wages, and what employers want from their workmen most of all is a low labor cost of manufacture.

These two conditions are not diametrically opposed to one another as would appear at first glance. On the contrary, they can be made to go together in all classes of work, without exception, and in the writer's judgment the existence or absence of these two elements forms the best index to either good or bad management.

This book is written mainly with the object of advocating high wages and low labor cost as the foundation of the best management, of pointing out the general principles which render it possible to maintain these conditions even under the most trying circumstances, and of indicating the various steps which the writer thinks should be taken in changing from a poor system to a better type of management.

The condition of high wages and low labor cost is far from being accepted either by the average manager or the average workman as a practical working basis. It is safe to say that the majority of employers have a feeling of satisfaction when their workmen are receiving lower wages than those of their competitors. On the other hand very many workmen feel contented if they find themselves doing the same amount of work per day as other similar workmen do and yet are getting more pay for it. Employers and workmen alike should look upon both of these conditions with apprehension, as either of them are sure, in the long run, to lead to trouble and loss for both parties.

Through unusual personal influence and energy, or more frequently through especial conditions which are but temporary, such as dull times when there is a surplus of labor, a superintendent may succeed in getting men to work extra hard for ordinary wages. After the men, however, realize that this is the case and an opportunity comes for them to change these conditions, in their reaction against what they believe unjust treatment they are almost sure to lean so far in the other direction as to do an equally great injustice to their employer.

On the other hand, the men who use the opportunity offered by a scarcity of labor to exact wages higher than the average of their class, without doing more than the average work in return, are merely laying up trouble for themselves in the long run. They grow accustomed to a high rate of living and expenditure, and when the inevitable turn comes and they are either thrown out of employment or forced to accept low wages, they are the losers by the whole transaction.

The only condition which contains the elements of stability and permanent satisfaction is that in which both employer and employees are doing as well or better than their competitors are likely to do, and this in nine cases out of ten means high wages and low labor cost, and both parties should be equally anxious for these conditions to prevail. With them the employer can hold his own with his competitors at all times and secure sufficient work to keep his men busy even in dull times. Without them both parties may do well enough in busy times, but both parties are likely to suffer when work becomes scarce.

6

The possibility of coupling high wages with a low labor cost rests mainly upon the enormous difference between the amount of work which a first-class man can do under favorable circumstances and the work which is actually done by the average man.

That there is a difference between the average and the first-class man is known to all employers, but that the first-class man can do in most cases from two to four times as much as is done by an average man is known to but few, and is fully realized only by those who have made a thorough and scientific study of the possibilities of men.

The writer has found this enormous difference between the first-class and average man to exist in all of the trades and branches of labor which he has investigated, and these cover a large field, as he, together with several of his friends, has been engaged with more than usual opportunities for thirty years past in carefully and systematically studying this subject.

The difference in the output of first-class and average men is as little realized by the workmen as by their employers. The first-class men know that they can do more work than the average, but they have rarely made any careful study of the matter. And the writer has over and over again found them utterly incredulous when he informed them, after close observation and study, how much they were able to do. In fact, in most cases when first told that they are able to do two or three times as much as they have done they take it as a joke and will not believe that one is in earnest.

It must be distinctly understood that in referring to the possibilities of a first-class man the writer does not mean what he can do when on a spurt or when he is over-exerting himself, but what a good man can keep up for a long term of years without injury to his health. It is a pace under which men become happier and thrive.

7

The second and equally interesting fact upon which the possibility of coupling high wages with low labor cost rests, is that first-class men are not only willing but glad to work at their maximum speed, providing they are paid from 30 to 100 per cent more than the average of their trade.

The exact percentage by which the wages must be increased in order to make them work to their maximum is not a subject to be theorized over, settled by boards of directors sitting in solemn conclave, nor voted upon by trades unions. It is a fact inherent in human nature and has only been determined through the slow and difficult process of trial and error.

The writer has found, for example, after making many mistakes above and below the proper mark, that to get the maximum output for ordinary shop work requiring neither especial brains, very close application, skill, nor extra hard work, such, for instance, as the more ordinary kinds of routine machine shop work, it is necessary to pay about 30 per cent more than the average. For ordinary day labor requiring little brains or special skill, but calling for strength, severe bodily exertion, and fatigue, it is necessary to pay from 50 per cent to 60 per cent above the average. For work requiring especial skill or brains, coupled with close application, but without severe bodily exertion, such as the more difficult and delicate machinist's work, from 70 per cent to 80 per cent beyond the average. And for work requiring skill, brains, close application, strength, and severe bodily exertion, such, for instance, as that involved in operating a well run steam hammer doing miscellaneous work, from 80 per cent to 100 per cent beyond the average.

There are plenty of good men ready to do their best for the above percentages of increase, but if the endeavor is made to get the right men to work at this maximum for less than the above increase, it will be found that most of them will prefer their old rate of speed with the lower pay. After trying the high speed piece work for a while they will one after another throw up their

8

jobs and return to the old day work conditions. Men will not work at their best unless assured a good liberal increase, which must be permanent.

It is the writer's judgment, on the other hand, that for their own good it is as important that workmen should not be very much over-paid, as it is that they should not be under-paid. If over-paid, many will work irregularly and tend to become more or less shiftless, extravagant, arid dissipated. It does not do for most men to get rich too fast. The writer's observation, however, would lead him to the conclusion that most men tend to become more instead of less thrifty when they receive the proper increase for an extra hard day's work, as, for example, the percentages of increase referred to above. They live rather better, begin to save money, become more sober, and work more steadily. And this certainly forms one of the strongest reasons for advocating this type of management.

In referring to high wages and low labor cost as fundamental in good management, the writer is most desirous not to be misunderstood.

By high wages he means wages which are high only with relation to the average of the class to which the man belongs and which are paid only to those who do much more or better work than the average of their class. He would not for an instant advocate the use of a high-priced tradesman to do the work which could be done by a trained laborer or a lower-priced man. No one would think of using a fine trotter to draw a grocery wagon nor a Percheron to do the work of a little mule. No more should a mechanic be allowed to do work for which a trained laborer can be used, and the writer goes so far as to say that almost any job that is repeated over and over again, however great skill and dexterity it may require, providing there is enough of it to occupy a man throughout a considerable part of the year, should be done by a trained laborer and not by a mechanic. A man with only the intelligence of an average laborer can be taught to do the most difficult and delicate work if it is repeated enough times; and his lower mental caliber renders him more fit than the mechanic to stand the monotony of repetition. It would seem to be the duty of employers, therefore, both in their own interest and in that of their employees, to see that each workman is given as far as possible the highest class of work for which his brains and physique fit him. A man, however, whose mental caliber and education do not fit him to become a good mechanic (and that grade of man is the one referred to as belonging to the "laboring class"), when he is trained to do some few especial jobs, which were formerly done by mechanics, should not expect to be paid the wages of a mechanic. He should get more than the average laborer, but less than a mechanic; thus insuring high wages to the workman, and low labor cost to the employer, and in this way making it most apparent to both that their interests are mutual.

To summarize, then, what the aim in each establishment should be:

(a) That each workman should be given as far as possible the highest grade of work for which his ability and physique fit him.

(b) That each workman should be called upon to turn out the maximum amount of work which a first-rate man of his class can do and thrive.

(c) That each workman, when he works at the best pace of a first-class man, should be paid from 30 per cent to 100 per cent according to the nature of the work which he does, beyond the average of his class.

And this means high wages and a low labor cost. These conditions not only serve the best interests of the employer, but they tend to raise each workman to the highest level which he is fitted to attain by making him use his best faculties, forcing him to become and remain ambitious and energetic, and giving him sufficient pay to live better than in the past.

Under these conditions the writer has seen many first-class men developed who otherwise would have remained second or third class all of their lives.

Is not the presence or absence of these conditions the best indication that any system of management is either well or badly applied? And in considering the relative merits of different types of management, is not that system the best which will establish these conditions with the greatest certainty, precision, and speed?

In comparing the management of manufacturing and engineering companies by this standard, it is surprising to see how far they fall short. Few of those which are best organized have attained even approximately the maximum output of first-class men.

Many of them are paying much higher prices per piece than are required to secure the maximum product while owing to a bad system, lack of exact knowledge of the time required to do work, and mutual suspicion and misunderstanding between employers and men, the output per man is so small that the men receive little if any more than average wages, both sides being evidently the losers thereby. The chief causes which produce this loss to both parties are: First (and by far the most important), the profound ignorance of employers and their foremen as to the time in which various kinds of work should be done, and this ignorance is shared largely by the workmen. Second: The indifference of the employers and their ignorance as to the proper system of management to adopt and the method of applying it, and further their indifference as to the individual character, worth, and welfare of their men. On the part of the men the greatest obstacle to the attainment of this standard is the

11

slow pace which they adopt, or the loafing or "soldiering,'" marking time, as it is called.

This loafing or soldiering proceeds from two causes. First, from the natural instinct and tendency of men to take it easy, which may be called natural soldiering. Second, from more intricate second thought and reasoning caused by their relations with other men, which may be called systematic soldiering. There is no question that the tendency of the average man (in all walks of life) is toward working at a slow, easy gait, and that it is only after a good deal of thought and observation on his part or as a result of example, conscience, or external pressure that he takes a more rapid pace.

There are, of course, men of unusual energy, vitality, and ambition who naturally choose the fastest gait, set up their own standards, and who will work hard, even though it may be against their best interests. But these few uncommon men only serve by affording a contrast to emphasize the tendency of the average.

This common tendency to "take it easy" is greatly increased by bringing a number of men together on similar work and at a uniform standard rate of pay by the day.

Under this plan the better men gradually but surely slow down their gait to that of the poorest and least efficient. When a naturally energetic man works for a few days beside a lazy one, the logic of the situation is unanswerable: "Why should I work hard when that lazy fellow gets the same pay that I do and does only half as much work?"

A careful time study of men working under these conditions will disclose facts which are ludicrous as well as pitiable.

To illustrate: The writer has timed a naturally energetic workman who, while going and coming from work, would walk at a speed of from three to four miles per hour, and not infrequently trot home after a day's work. On arriving at his work he would immediately slow down to a speed of about one mile an hour. When, for example, wheeling a loaded wheelbarrow he would go at a good fast pace even up hill in order to be as short a time as possible under load, and immediately on the return walk slow down to a mile an hour, improving every opportunity for delay short of actually sitting down. In order to be sure not to do more than his lazy neighbor he would actually tire himself in his effort to go slow.

These men were working under a foreman of good reputation and one highly thought of by his employer who, when his attention was called to this state of things, answered: "Well, I can keep them from sitting down, but the devil can't make them get a move on while they are at work."

The natural laziness of men is serious, but by far the greatest evil from which both workmen and employers are suffering is the systematic soldiering which is almost universal under all of the ordinary schemes of management and which results from a careful study on the part of the workmen of what they think will promote their best interests.

The writer was much interested recently to hear one small but experienced golf caddy boy of twelve explaining to a green caddy who had shown special energy and interest the necessity of going slow and lagging behind his man when he came up to the ball, showing him that since they were paid by the hour, the faster they went the less money they got, and finally telling him that if he went too fast the other boys would give him a licking.

This represents a type of systematic soldiering which is not, however, very serious, since it is done with the knowledge of the employer, who can quite easily break it up if he wishes.

The greater part of the systematic soldiering, however, is done by the men with the deliberate object of keeping their employers ignorant of how fast work can be done.

So universal is soldiering for this purpose, that hardly a competent workman can be found in a large establishment, whether he works by the day or on piece work, contract work or under any of the ordinary systems of compensating labor, who does not devote a considerable part of his time to studying just how slowly he can work and still convince his employer that he is going at a good pace.

The causes for this are, briefly, that practically all employers determine upon a maximum sum which they feel it is right for each of their classes of employees to earn per day, whether their men work by the day or piece.

Each workman soon finds out about what this figure is for his particular case, and he also realizes that when his employer is convinced that a man is capable of doing more work than he has done, he will find sooner or later some way of compelling him to do it with little or no increase of pay.

Employers derive their knowledge of how much of a given class of work can be done in a day from either their own experience, which has frequently grown hazy with age, from casual and unsystematic observation of their men, or at best from records which are kept, showing, the quickest time in which each job has been done. In many cases the employer will feel almost certain that a given job can be done faster than it has been, but he rarely cares to take the drastic measures necessary to force men to do it in the quickest time, unless he has an actual record, proving conclusively how fast the work can be done.

It evidently becomes for each man's interest, then, to see that no job is done faster than it has been in the past. The younger and less experienced men are taught this by their elders, and all possible persuasion and social pressure is brought to bear upon the greedy and selfish men to keep them from making new records which result in temporarily increasing their wages, while all those who come after them are made to work harder for the same old pay.

Under the best day work of the ordinary type, when accurate records are kept of the amount of work done by each man and of his efficiency, and when each man's wages are raised as he improves, and those who fail to rise to a certain standard are discharged and a fresh supply of carefully selected men are given work in their places, both the natural loafing and systematic soldiering can be largely broken up. This can be done, however, only when the men are thoroughly convinced that there is no intention of establishing piece work even in the remote future, and it is next to impossible to make men believe this when the work is of such a nature that they believe piece work to be practicable. In most cases their fear of making a record which will be used as a basis for piece work will cause them to soldier as much as they dare.

It is, however, under piece work that the art of systematic soldiering is thoroughly developed. After a workman has had the price per piece of the work he is doing lowered two or three times as a result of his having worked harder and increased his output, he is likely to entirely lose sight of his employer's side of the case and to become imbued with a grim determination to have no more cuts if soldiering can prevent it. Unfortunately for the character of the workman, soldiering involves a deliberate attempt to mislead and deceive his employer, and thus upright and straight-forward workmen are compelled to become more or less hypocritical. The employer is soon looked upon as an antagonist, if not as an enemy, and the mutual confidence which should exist between a leader and his men, the enthusiasm, the feeling that they are all working for the same end and will share in the results, is entirely lacking.

The feeling of antagonism under the ordinary piecework system becomes in many cases so marked on the part of the men that any proposition made by their employers, however reasonable, is looked upon with suspicion. Soldiering becomes such a fixed habit that men will frequently take pains to restrict the product of machines which they are running when even a large increase in output would involve no more work on their part.

On work which is repeated over and over again and the volume of which is sufficient to permit it, the plan of making a contract with a competent workman to do a certain class of work and allowing him to employ his own men subject to strict limitations, is successful.

As a rule, the fewer the men employed by the contactor and the smaller the variety of the work, the greater will be the success under the contract system, the reason for this being that the contractor, under the spur of financial necessity, makes personally so close a study of the quickest time in which the work can be done that soldiering on the part of his men becomes difficult and the best of them teach laborers or lower-priced helpers to do the work formerly done by mechanics.

The objections to the contract system are that the machine tools used by the contractor are apt to deteriorate rapidly, his chief interest being to get a large output, whether the tools are properly cared for or not, and that through the ignorance and inexperience of the contractor in handling men, his employees are frequently unjustly treated.

These disadvantages are, however, more than counterbalanced by the comparative absence of soldiering on the part of the men.

The greatest objection to this system is the soldiering which the contractor himself does in many cases, so as to secure a good price for his next contract.

It is not at all unusual for a contractor to restrict the output of his own men and to refuse to adopt improvements in machines, appliances, or methods while in the midst of a contract, knowing that his next contract price will be lowered in direct proportion to the profits which he has made and the improvements introduced.

Under the contract system, however, the relations between employers and men are much more agreeable and normal than under piece work, and it is to be regretted that owing to the nature of the work done in most shops this system is not more generally applicable.

The writer quotes as follows from his paper on "A Piece Rate System," read in 1895, before The American Society of Mechanical Engineers:

"Cooperation, or profit sharing, has entered the mind of every student of the subject as one of the possible and most attractive solutions of the problem; and there have been certain instances, both in England and France, of at least a partial success of cooperative experiments.

"So far as I know, however, these trials have been made either in small towns, remote from the manufacturing centers, or in industries which in many respects are not subject to ordinary manufacturing conditions.

"Cooperative experiments have failed, and, I think, are generally destined to fail, for several reasons, the first and most important of which is, that no form of cooperation has yet been devised in which each individual is allowed free scope for his personal ambition. Personal ambition always has been and will remain a more powerful incentive to exertion than a desire for the general welfare. The few misplaced drones, who do the loafing and share equally in the profits with the rest, under cooperation are sure to drag the better men down toward their level.

"The second and almost equally strong reason for failure lies in the remoteness of the reward. The average workman (I don't say all men) cannot look forward to a profit which is six months or a year away. The nice time which they are sure to have today, if they take things easily, proves more attractive than hard work, with a possible reward to be shared with others six months later.

"Other and formidable difficulties in the path of cooperation are, the equitable division of the profits, and the fact that, while workmen are always ready to share the profits, they are neither able nor willing to share the losses. Further than this, in many cases, it is neither right nor just that they should share either in the profits or the losses, since these may be due in great part to causes entirely beyond their influence or control, and to which they do not contribute."

Of all the ordinary systems of management in use (in which no accurate scientific study of the time problem is undertaken, and no carefully measured tasks are assigned to the men which must be accomplished in a given time) the best is the plan fundamentally originated by Mr. Henry R. Towne, and improved and made practical by Mr. F. A. Halsey. This plan is described in papers read by Mr. Towne before The American Society of Mechanical Engineers in 1886, and by Mr. Halsey in 1891, and has since been criticized and ably defended in a series of articles appearing in the "American Machinist."

The Towne-Halsey plan consists in recording the quickest time in which a job has been done, and fixing this as a standard. If the workman succeeds in doing the job in a shorter time, he is still paid his same wages per hour for the time he works on the job, and in addition is given a premium for having worked faster, consisting of from one-quarter to one-half the difference between the wages earned and the wages originally paid when the job was done in standard time. Mr. Halsey recommends the payment of one third of the difference as the best premium for most cases. The difference between this system and ordinary piece work is that the workman on piece work gets the whole of the difference between the actual time of a job and the standard time, while under the Towne-Halsey plan he gets only a fraction of this difference.

It is not unusual to hear the Towne-Halsey plan referred to as practically the same as piece work. This is far from the truth, for while the difference between the two does not appear to a casual observer to be great, and the general principles of the two seem to be the same, still we all know that success or failure in many cases hinges upon small differences.

In the writer's judgment, the Towne-Halsey plan is a great invention, and, like many other great inventions, its value lies in its simplicity.

This plan has already been successfully adopted by a large number of establishments, and has resulted in giving higher wages to many workmen, accompanied by a lower labor cost to the employer, and at the same time materially improving their relations by lessening the feeling of antagonism between the two.

This system is successful because it diminishes soldiering, and this rests entirely upon the fact that since the workman only receives say one-third of the increase in pay that he would get under corresponding conditions on piece work, there is not the same temptation for the employer to cut prices.

After this system has been in operation for a year or two, if no cuts in prices have been made, the tendency of the men to soldier on that portion of the work which is being done under the system is diminished, although it does not entirely cease. On the other hand, the tendency of the men to soldier on new work which is started, and on such portions as are still done on day work, is even greater under the Towne-Halsey plan than under piece work.

To illustrate: Workmen, like the rest of mankind, are more strongly influenced by object lessons than by theories. The effect on men of such an object lesson as the following will be apparent. Suppose that two men, named respectively Smart and

19

Honest, are at work by the day and receive the same pay, say 20 cents per hour. Each of these men is given a new piece of work which could be done in one hour. Smart does his job in four hours (and it is by no means unusual for men to soldier to this extent). Honest does his in one and one-half hours.

Now, when these two jobs start on this basis under the Towne-Halsey plan and are ultimately done in one hour each, Smart receives for his job 20 cents per hour + a premium of 20 cents = a total of 40 cents. Honest receives for his job 20 cents per hour + a premium of 3 1/8 cents = a total of 23 1/8 cents.

Most of the men in the shop will follow the example of Smart rather than that of Honest and will "soldier" to the extent of three or four hundred per cent if allowed to do so. The Towne-Halsey system shares with ordinary piece work then, the greatest evil of the latter, namely that its very foundation rests upon deceit, and under both of these systems there is necessarily, as we have seen, a great lack of justice and equality in the starting-point of different jobs.

Some of the rates will have resulted from records obtained when a first-class man was working close to his maximum speed, while others will be based on the performance of a poor man at one-third or one quarter speed.

The injustice of the very foundation of the system is thus forced upon the workman every day of his life, and no man, however kindly disposed he may be toward his employer, can fail to resent this and be seriously influenced by it in his work. These systems are, therefore, of necessity slow and irregular in their operation in reducing costs. They "drift" gradually toward an increased output, but under them the attainment of the maximum output of a first-class man is almost impossible.

Objection has been made to the use of the word "drifting" in this connection. It is used absolutely without any intention of slurring the Towne-Halsey system or in the least detracting from its true merit.

It appears to me, however, that "drifting" very accurately describes it, for the reason that the management, having turned over the entire control of the speed problem to the men, the latter being influenced by their prejudices and whims, drift sometimes in one direction and sometimes in another; but on the whole, sooner or later, under the stimulus of the premium, move toward a higher rate of speed. This drifting, accompanied as it is by the irregularity and uncertainty both as to the final result which will be attained and as to how long it will take to reach this end, is in marked contrast to the distinct goal which is always kept in plain sight of both parties under task management, and the clear-cut directions which leave no doubt as to the means which are to be employed nor the time in which the work must be done; and these elements constitute the fundamental difference between the two systems. Mr. Halsey, in objecting to the use of the word "drifting" as describing his system, has referred to the use of his system in England in connection with a "rate-fixing" or planning department, and quotes as follows from his paper to show that he contemplated control of the speed of the work by the management:

"On contract work undertaken for the first time the method is the same except that the premium is based on the estimated time for the execution of the work."

In making this claim Mr. Halsey appears to have entirely lost sight of the real essence of the two plans. It is task management which is in use in England, not the Towne-Halsey system; and in the above quotation Mr. Halsey describes not his system but a type of task management, in which the men are paid a premium for carrying out the directions given them by the management.

There is no doubt that there is more or less confusion in the minds of many of those who have read about the task

21

management and the Towne-Halsey system. This extends also to those who are actually using and working under these systems. This is practically true in England, where in some cases task management is actually being used under the name of the "Premium Plan." It would therefore seem desirable to indicate once again and in a little different way the essential difference between the two.

The one element which the Towne-Halsey system and task management have in common is that both recognize the all-important fact that workmen cannot be induced to work extra hard without receiving extra pay. Under both systems the men who succeed are daily and automatically, as it were, paid an extra premium. The payment of this daily premium forms such a characteristic feature in both systems, and so radically differentiates these systems from those which were in use before, that people are apt to look upon this one element as the essence of both systems and so fail to recognize the more important, underlying principles upon which the success of each of them is based.

In their essence, with the one exception of the payment of a daily premium, the systems stand at the two opposite extremes in the field of management; and it is owing to the distinctly radical, though opposite, positions taken by them that each one owes its success; and it seems to me a matter of importance that this should be understood. In any executive work which involves the cooperation of two different men or parties, where both parties have anything like equal power or voice in its direction, there is almost sure to be a certain amount of bickering, quarreling, and vacillation, and the success of the enterprise suffers accordingly. If, however, either one of the parties has the entire direction, the enterprise will progress consistently and probably harmoniously, even although the wrong one of the two parties may be in control.

Broadly speaking, in the field of management there are two

parties—the superintendents, etc., on one side and the men on the other, and the main questions at issue are the speed and accuracy with which the work shall be done. Up to the time that task management was introduced in the Midvale Steel Works, it can be fairly said that under the old systems of management the men and the management had about equal weight in deciding how fast the work should be done. Shop records showing the quickest time in which each job had been done and more or less shrewd guessing being the means on which the management depended for bargaining with and coercing the men; and deliberate soldiering for the purpose of misinforming the management being the weapon used by the men in self-defense. Under the old system the incentive was entirely lacking which is needed to induce men to cooperate heartily with the management in increasing the speed with which work is turned out. It is chiefly due, under the old systems, to this divided control of the speed with which the work shall be done that such an amount of bickering, quarreling, and often hard feeling exists between the two sides.

The essence of task management lies in the fact that the control of the speed problem rests entirely with the management; and, on the other hand, the true strength of the Towne-Halsey system rests upon the fact that under it the question of speed is settled entirely by the men without interference on the part of the management. Thus in both cases, though from diametrically opposite causes, there is undivided control, and this is the chief element needed for harmony.

The writer has seen many jobs successfully nursed in several of our large and well managed establishments under these drifting systems, for a term of ten to fifteen years, at from one-third to one-quarter speed. The workmen, in the meanwhile, apparently enjoyed the confidence of their employers, and in many cases the employers not only suspected the deceit, but felt quite sure of it.

The great defect, then, common to all the ordinary systems of management (including the Towne-Halsey system, the best of this class) is that their starting-point, their very foundation, rests upon ignorance and deceit, and that throughout their whole course in the one element which is most vital both to employer and workmen, namely, the speed at which work is done, they are allowed to drift instead of being intelligently directed and controlled.

The writer has found, through an experience of thirty years, covering a large variety in manufactures, as well as in the building trades, structural and engineering work, that it is not only practicable but comparatively easy to obtain, through a systematic and scientific time study, exact information as to how much of any given kind of work either a first-class or an average man can do in a day, and with this information as a foundation, he has over and over again seen the fact demonstrated that workmen of all classes are not only willing, but glad to give up all idea of soldiering, and devote all of their energies to turning out the maximum work possible, providing they are sure of a suitable permanent reward.

With accurate time knowledge as a basis, surprisingly large results can be obtained under any scheme of management from day work up; there is no question that even ordinary day work resting upon this foundation will give greater satisfaction than any of the systems in common use, standing as they do upon soldiering as a basis.

To many of the readers of this book both the fundamental objects to be aimed at, namely, high wages with low labor cost, and the means advocated by the writer for attaining this end; namely, accurate time study, will appear so theoretical and so far outside of the range of their personal observation and experience that it would seem desirable, before proceeding farther, to give a brief illustration of what has been accomplished in this line.

The writer chooses from among a large variety of trades to

which these principles have been applied, the yard labor handling raw materials in the works of the Bethlehem Steel Company at South Bethlehem, Pa., not because the results attained there have been greater than in many other instances, but because the case is so elementary that the results are evidently due to no other cause than thorough time study as a basis, followed by the application of a few simple principles with which all of us are familiar.

In almost all of the other more complicated cases the large increase in output is due partly to the actual physical changes, either in the machines or small tools and appliances, which a preliminary time study almost always shows to be necessary, so that for purposes of illustration the simple case chosen is the better, although the gain made in the more complicated cases is none the less legitimately due to the system.

Up to the spring of the year 1899, all of the materials in the yard of the Bethlehem Steel Company had been handled by gangs of men working by the day, and under the foremanship of men who had themselves formerly worked at similar work as laborers. Their management was about as good as the average of similar work, although it was bad all of the men being paid the ruling wages of laborers in this section of the country, namely, $1.15 per day, the only means of encouraging or disciplining them being either talking to them or discharging them; occasionally, however, a man was selected from among these men and given a better class of work with slightly higher wages in some of the companies' shops, and this had the effect of slightly stimulating them. From four to six hundred men were employed on this class of work throughout the year.

The work of these men consisted mainly of unloading from railway cars and shoveling on to piles, and from these piles again loading as required, the raw materials used in running three blast furnaces and seven large open-hearth furnaces, such as ore of various kinds, varying from fine, gravelly ore to that

25

which comes in large lumps, coke, limestone, special pig, sand, etc., unloading hard and soft coal for boilers gas-producers, etc., and also for storage and again loading the stored coal as required for use, loading the pig-iron produced at the furnaces for shipment, for storage, and for local use, and handling billets, etc., produced by the rolling mills. The work covered a large variety as laboring work goes, and it was not usual to keep a man continuously at the same class of work.

Before undertaking the management of these men, the writer was informed that they were steady workers, but slow and phlegmatic, and that nothing would induce them to work fast.

The first step was to place an intelligent, college-educated man in charge of progress in this line. This man had not before handled this class of labor, although he understood managing workmen. He was not familiar with the methods pursued by the writer, but was soon taught the art of determining how much work a first-class man can do in a day. This was done by timing with a stop watch a first-class man while he was working fast. The best way to do this, in fact almost the only way in which the timing can be done with certainty, is to divide the man's work into its elements and time each element separately. For example, in the case of a man loading pig-iron on to a car, the elements should be: (a) picking up the pig from the ground or pile (time in hundredths of a minute); (b) walking with it on a level (time per foot walked); (c) walking with it up an incline to car (time per foot walked); (d) throwing the pig down (time in hundredths of a minute), or laying it on a pile (time in hundredths of a minute); (e) walking back empty to get a load (time per foot walked).

In case of important elements which were to enter into a number of rates, a large number of observations were taken when practicable on different first-class men, and at different times, and they were averaged.

The most difficult elements to time and decide upon in this, as in

26

most cases, are the percentage of the day required for rest, and the time to allow for accidental or unavoidable delays.

In the case of the yard labor at Bethlehem, each class of work was studied as above, each element being timed separately, and, in addition, a record was kept in many cases of the total amount of work done by the man in a day. The record of the gross work of the man (who is being timed) is, in most cases, not necessary after the observer is skilled in his work. As the Bethlehem time observer was new to this work, the gross time was useful in checking his detailed observations and so gradually educating him and giving him confidence in the new methods.

The writer had so many other duties that his personal help was confined to teaching the proper methods and approving the details of the various changes which were in all cases outlined in written reports before being carried out.

As soon as a careful study had been made of the time elements entering into one class of work, a single first-class workman was picked out and started on ordinary piece work on this job. His task required him to do between three and one-half and four times as much work in a day as had been done in the past on an average.

Between twelve and thirteen tons of pig-iron per man had been carried from a pile on the ground, up an inclined plank, and loaded on to a gondola car by the average pig-iron handler while working by the day. The men in doing this work had worked in gangs of from five to twenty men.

The man selected from one of these gangs to make the first start under the writer's system was called upon to load on piece work from forty-five to forty-eight tons (2,240 lbs. each) per day.

He regarded this task as an entirely fair one, and earned on an average, from the start, $1.85 per day, which was 60 per cent more than he had been paid by the day. This man happened to

27

be considerably lighter than the average good workman at this class of work. He weighed about 130 pounds. He proved however, to be especially well suited to this job, and was kept at it steadily throughout the time that the writer was in Bethlehem, and some years later was still at the same work.

Being the first piece work started in the works, it excited considerable opposition, both on the part of the workmen and of several of the leading men in the town, their opposition being based mainly on the old fallacy that if piece work proved successful a great many men would be thrown out of work, and that thereby not only the workmen but the whole town would suffer.

One after another of the new men who were started singly on this job were either persuaded or intimidated into giving it up. In many cases they were given other work by those interested in preventing piece work, at wages higher than the ruling wages. In the meantime, however, the first man who started on the work earned steadily $1.85 per day, and this object lesson gradually wore out the concerted opposition, which ceased rather suddenly after about two months. From this time on there was no difficulty in getting plenty of good men who were anxious to start on piece work, and the difficulty lay in making with sufficient rapidity the accurate time study of the elementary operations or "unit times" which forms the foundation of this kind of piece work.

Throughout the introduction of piece work, when after a thorough time study a new section of the work was started, one man only was put on each new job, and not more than one man was allowed to work at it until he had demonstrated that the task set was a fair one by earning an average of $1.85 per day. After a few sections of the work had been started in this way, the complaint on the part of the better workmen was that they were not allowed to go on to piece work fast enough. It required about two years to transfer practically all of the yard labor from day to piece work. And the larger part of the transfer was made during the last six months of this time.

As stated above, the greater part of the time was taken up in studying "unit times," and this time study was greatly delayed by having successively the two leading men who had been trained to the work leave because they were offered much larger salaries elsewhere. The study of "unit times" for the yard labor took practically the time of two trained men for two years. Throughout this time the day and piece workers were under entirely separate and distinct management. The original foremen continued to manage the day work, and day and piece workers were never allowed to work together. Gradually the day work gang was diminished and the piece workers were increased as one section of work after another was transformed from the former to the latter.

Two elements which were important to the success of this work should be noted:

First, on the morning following each day's work, each workman was given a slip of paper informing him in detail just how much work he had done the day before, and the amount he had earned. This enabled him to measure his performance against his earnings while the details were fresh in his mind. Without this there would have been great dissatisfaction among those who failed to climb up to the task asked of them, and many would have gradually fallen off in their performance.

Second, whenever it was practicable, each man's work was measured by itself. Only when absolutely necessary was the work of two men measured up together and the price divided between them, and then care was taken to select two men of as nearly as possible the same capacity. Only on few occasions, and then upon special permission, signed by the writer, were more than two men allowed to work on gang work, dividing their

29

earnings between them. Gang work almost invariably results in a failing off in earnings and consequent dissatisfaction.

An interesting illustration of the desirability of individual piece work instead of gang work came to our attention at Bethlehem. Several of the best piece workers among the Bethlehem yard laborers were informed by their friends that a much higher price per ton was paid for shoveling ore in another works than the rate given at Bethlehem. After talking the matter over with the writer he advised them to go to the other works, which they accordingly did. In about a month they were all back at work in Bethlehem again, having found that at the other works they were obliged to work with a gang of men instead of on individual piece work, and that the rest of the gang worked so slowly that in spite of the high price paid per ton they earned much less than Bethlehem.

Table 1, on page 54, gives a summary of the work done by the piece-work laborers in handling raw materials, such as ores, anthracite and bituminous coal, coke, pig-iron, sand, limestone, cinder, scale, ashes, etc., in the works of the Bethlehem Steel Company, during the year ending April 30, 1900. This work consisted mainly in loading and unloading cars on arrival or departure from the works, and for local transportation, and was done entirely by hand, i.e., without the use of cranes or other machinery.

The greater part of the credit for making the accurate time study and actually managing the men on this work should be given to Mr. A. B. Wadleigh, the writer's assistant in this section at that time.

TABLE 1. -SHOWING RELATIVE COST OF YARD LABOR UNDER TASK PIECE WORK AND OLD STYLE DAY WORK

[Transcriber's note — table 1 omitted]

When the writer left the steel works, the Bethlehem piece

30

workers were the finest body of picked laborers that he has ever seen together. They were practically all first-class men, because in each case the task which they were called upon to perform was such that only a first-class man could do it. The tasks were all purposely made so severe that not more than one out of five laborers (perhaps even a smaller percentage than this) could keep up.

[Footnotes to table 1]

1) It was our intention to fix piece work rates which should enable first-class workmen to average about 60 per cent more than they had been earning on day work, namely $1.85 per day. A year's average shows them to have earned $1.88 per day, or three cents per man per day more than we expected—an error of 1 6/10 per cent.

2) The piece workers handled on an average 3 56/100 times as many tons per day as the day workers.

[end footnotes to table 1]

It was clearly understood by each newcomer as he went to work that unless he was able to average at least $1.85 per day he would have to make way for another man who could do so. As a result, first-class men from all over that part of the country, who were in most cases earning from $1.05 to $1.15 per day, were anxious to try their hands at earning $1.85 per day. If they succeeded they were naturally contented, and if they failed they left, sorry that they were unable to maintain the proper pace, but with no hard feelings either toward the system or the management. Throughout the time that the writer was there, labor was as scarce and as difficult to get as it ever has been in the history of this country, and yet there was always a surplus of first-class men ready to leave other jobs and try their hand at Bethlehem piece work.

Perhaps the most notable difference between these men and

ordinary piece workers lay in their changed mental attitude toward their employers and their work, and in the total absence of soldiering on their part. The ordinary piece worker would have spent a considerable part of his time in deciding just how much his employer would allow him to earn without cutting prices and in then trying to come as close as possible to this figure, while carefully guarding each job so as to keep the management from finding out how fast it really could be done. These men, however, were faced with a new but very simple and straightforward proposition, namely, am I a first-class laborer or not? Each man felt that if he belonged in the first class all he had to do was to work at his best and he would be paid sixty per cent more than he had been paid in the past. Each piece work price was accepted by the men without question. They never bargained over nor complained about rates, and there was no occasion to do so, since they were all equally fair, and called for almost exactly the same amount of work and fatigue per dollar of wages.

A careful inquiry into the condition of these men when away from work developed the fact that out of the whole gang only two were said to be drinking men. This does not, of course, imply that many of them did not take an occasional drink. The fact is that a steady drinker would find it almost impossible to keep up with the pace which was set, so that they were practically all sober. Many if not most of them were saving money, and they all lived better than they had before. The results attained under this system were most satisfactory both to employer and workmen, and show in a convincing way the possibility of uniting high wages with a low labor cost.

This is virtually a labor union of first-class men, who are united together to secure the extra high wages, which belong to them by right and which in this case are begrudged them by none, and which will be theirs through dull times as well as periods of activity. Such a union commands the unqualified admiration and respect of all classes of the community; the respect equally of workmen, employers, political economists, and philanthropists. There are no dues for membership, since all of the expenses are paid by the company. The employers act as officers of the Union, to enforce its rules and keep its records, since the interests of the company are identical and bound up with those of the men. It is never necessary to plead with, or persuade men to join this Union, since the employers themselves organize it free of cost; the best workmen in the community are always anxious to belong to it. The feature most to be regretted about it is that the membership is limited.

The words "labor union" are, however, unfortunately so closely associated in the minds of most people with the idea of disagreement and strife between employers and men that it seems almost incongruous to apply them to this case. Is not this, however, the ideal "labor union," with character and special ability of a high order as the only qualifications for membership.

It is a curious fact that with the people to whom the writer has described this system, the first feeling, particularly among those more philanthropically inclined, is one of pity for the inferior workmen who lost their jobs in order to make way for the first-class men. This sympathy is entirely misplaced. There was such a demand for labor at the time that no workman was obliged to be out of work for more than a day or two, and so the poor workmen were practically as well off as ever. The feeling, instead of being one of pity for the inferior workmen, should be one of congratulation and rejoicing that many first-class men—who through unfortunate circumstances had never had the opportunity of proving their worth—at last were given the chance to earn high wages and become prosperous.

What the writer wishes particularly to emphasize is that this whole system rests upon an accurate and scientific study of unit times, which is by far the most important element in scientific management. With it, greater and more permanent results can be

33

attained even under ordinary day work or piece work than can be reached under any of the more elaborate systems without it.

In 1895 the writer read a paper before The American Society of Mechanical Engineers entitled "A Piece Rate System." His chief object in writing it was to advocate the study of unit times as the foundation of good management. Unfortunately, he at the same time described the "differential rate" system of piece work, which had been introduced by him in the Midvale Steel Works. Although he called attention to the fact that the latter was entirely of secondary importance, the differential rate was widely discussed in the journals of this country and abroad while practically nothing was said about the study of "unit times." Thirteen members of the Society discussed the piece rate system at length, and only two briefly referred to the study of the "unit times."

The writer most sincerely trusts that his leading object in writing this book will not be overlooked, and that scientific time study will receive the attention which it merits. Bearing in mind the Bethlehem yard labor as an illustration of the application of the study of unit times as the foundation of success in management, the following would seem to him a fair comparison of the older methods with the more modern plan.

For each job there is the quickest time in which it can be done by a first-class man. This time may be called the "quickest time," or the "standard time" for the job. Under all the ordinary systems, this "quickest time" is more or less completely shrouded in mist. In most cases, however, the workman is nearer to it and sees it more clearly than the employer.

Under ordinary piece work the management watch every indication given them by the workmen as to what the "quickest time" is for each job, and endeavor continually to force the men toward this "standard time," while the workmen constantly use every effort to prevent this from being done and to lead the management in the wrong direction. In spite of this conflict, however, the "standard time" is gradually approached.

Under the Towne-Halsey plan the management gives up all direct effort to reach this "quickest time," but offers mild inducements to the workmen to do so, and turns over the whole enterprise to them. The workmen, peacefully as far as the management is concerned, but with considerable pulling and hauling among themselves, and without the assistance of a trained guiding hand, drift gradually and slowly in the direction of the "standard time," but rarely approach it closely.

With accurate time study as a basis, the "quickest time" for each job is at all times in plain sight of both employers and workmen, and is reached with accuracy, precision, and speed, both sides pulling hard in the same direction under the uniform simple and just agreement that whenever a first-class man works his best he will receive from 30 to 100 per cent more than the average of his trade.

Probably a majority of the attempts that are made to radically change the organization of manufacturing companies result in a loss of money to the company, failure to bring about the change sought for, and a return to practically the original organization. The reason for this being that there are but few employers who look upon management as an art, and that they go at a difficult task without either having understood or appreciated the time required for organization or its cost, the troubles to be met with, or the obstacles to be overcome, and without having studied the means to be employed in doing so.

Before starting to make any changes in the organization of a company the following matters should be carefully considered: First, the importance of choosing the general type of management best suited to the particular case. Second, that in all cases money must be spent, and in many cases a great deal of money, before the changes are completed which result in lowering cost. Third, that it takes time to reach any result worth aiming at. Fourth, the importance of making changes in their proper order, and that unless the right steps are taken, and taken in their proper sequence, there is great danger from deterioration in the quality of the output and from serious troubles with the workmen, often resulting in strikes.

As to the type of management to be ultimately aimed at, before any changes whatever are made, it is necessary, or at least highly desirable, that the most careful consideration should be given to the type to be chosen; and once a scheme is decided upon it should be carried forward step by step without wavering or retrograding. Workmen will tolerate and even come to have great respect for one change after another made in logical sequence and according to a consistent plan. It is most demoralizing, however, to have to recall a step once taken, whatever may be the cause, and it makes any further changes doubly difficult.

The choice must be made between some of the types of management in common use, which the writer feels are properly designated by the word "drifting," and the more modern scientific management based on an accurate knowledge of how long it should take to do the work. If, as is frequently the case, the managers of an enterprise find themselves so overwhelmed with other departments of the business that they can give but little thought to the management of the shop, then some one of the various "drifting" schemes should be adopted; and of these the writer believes the Towne-Halsey plan to be the best, since it drifts safely and peacefully though slowly in the right direction; yet under it the best results can never be reached. The fact, however, that managers are in this way overwhelmed by their work is the best proof that there is something radically wrong with the plan of their organization and in self defense they should take immediate steps toward a more thorough study of the art.

36

It is not at all generally realized that whatever system may be used, —providing a business is complex in its nature—the building up of an efficient organization is necessarily slow and sometimes very expensive. Almost all of the directors of manufacturing companies appreciate the economy of a thoroughly modern, up-to-date, and efficient plant, and are willing to pay for it. Very few of them, however, realize that the best organization, whatever its cost may be, is in many cases even more important than the plant; nor do they clearly realize that no kind of an efficient organization can be built up without spending money. The spending of money for good machinery appeals to them because they can see machines after they are bought; but putting money into anything so invisible, intangible, and to the average man so indefinite, as an organization seems almost like throwing it away.

There is no question that when the work to be done is at all complicated, a good organization with a poor plant will give better results than the best plant with a poor organization. One of the most successful manufacturers in this country was asked recently by a number of financiers whether he thought that the difference between one style of organization and another amounted to much providing the company had an up-to-date plant properly located. His answer was, "If I had to choose now between abandoning my present organization and burning down all of my plants which have cost me millions, I should choose the latter. My plants could be rebuilt in a short while with borrowed money, but I could hardly replace my organization in a generation."

Modern engineering can almost be called an exact science; each year removes it further from guess work and from rule-of-thumb methods and establishes it more firmly upon the foundation of fixed principles.

The writer feels that management is also destined to become more of an art, and that many of the, elements which are now

37

believed to be outside the field of exact knowledge will soon be standardized tabulated, accepted, and used, as are now many of the elements of engineering. Management will be studied as an art and will rest upon well recognized, clearly defined, and fixed principles instead of depending upon more or less hazy ideas received from a limited observation of the few organizations with which the individual may have come in contact. There will, of course, be various successful types, and the application of the underlying principles must be modified to suit each particular case. The writer has already indicated that he thinks the first object in management is to unite high wages with a low labor cost. He believes that this object can be most easily attained by the application of the following principles:

(a) A LARGE DAILY TASK. —Each man in the establishment, high or low, should daily have a clearly defined task laid out before him. This task should not in the least degree be vague nor indefinite, but should be circumscribed carefully and completely, and should not be easy to accomplish.

(b) STANDARD CONDITIONS. —Each man's task should call for a full day's work, and at the same time the workman should be given such standardized conditions and appliances as will enable him to accomplish his task with certainty.

(c) HIGH PAY FOR SUCCESS. —He should be sure of large pay when he accomplishes his task.

(d) LOSS IN CASE OF FAILURE. —When he fails he should be sure that sooner or later he will be the loser by it.

When an establishment has reached an advanced state of organization, in many cases a fifth element should be added, namely: the task should be made so difficult that it can only be accomplished by a first-class man.

There is nothing new nor startling about any of these principles and yet it will be difficult to find a shop in which they are not

38

daily violated over and over again. They call, however, for a greater departure from the ordinary types of organization than would at first appear. In the case, for instance, of a machine shop doing miscellaneous work, in order to assign daily to each man a carefully measured task, a special planning department is required to lay out all of the work at least one day ahead. All orders must be given to the men in detail in writing; and in order to lay out the next day's work and plan the entire progress of work through the shop, daily returns must be made by the men to the planning department in writing, showing just what has been done. Before each casting or forging arrives in the shop the exact route which it is to take from machine to machine should be laid out. An instruction card for each operation must be written out stating in detail just how each operation on every piece of work is to be done and the time required to do it, the drawing number, any special tools, jigs, or appliances required, etc. Before the four principles above referred to can be successfully applied it is also necessary in most shops to make important physical changes. All of the small details in the shop, which are usually regarded as of little importance and are left to be regulated according to the individual taste of the workman, or, at best, of the foreman, must be thoroughly and carefully standardized; such. details, for instance, as the care and tightening of the belts; the exact shape and quality of each cutting tool; the establishment of a complete tool room from which properly ground tools, as well as jigs, templates, drawings, etc., are issued under a good check system, etc.; and as a matter of importance (in fact, as the foundation of scientific management) an accurate study of unit times must be made by one or more men connected with the planning department, and each machine tool must be standardized and a table or slide rule constructed for it showing how to run it to the best advantage.

At first view the running of a planning department, together with the other innovations, would appear to involve a large amount of additional work and expense, and the most natural

39

question would be is whether the increased efficiency of the shop more than offsets this outlay? It must be borne in mind, however, that, with the exception of the study of unit times, there is hardly a single item of work done in the planning department which is not already being done in the shop. Establishing a planning department merely concentrates the planning and much other brainwork in a few men especially fitted for their task and trained in their especial lines, instead of having it done, as heretofore, in most cases by high priced mechanics, well fitted to work at their trades, but poorly trained for work more or less clerical in its nature.

There is a close analogy between the methods of modern engineering and this type of management. Engineering now centers in the drafting room as modern management does in the planning department. The new style engineering has all the appearance of complication and extravagance, with its multitude of drawings; the amount of study and work which is put into each detail; and its corps of draftsmen, all of whom would be sneered at by the old engineer as "non-producers." For the same reason, modern management, with its minute time study and a managing department in which each operation is carefully planned, with its many written orders and its apparent red tape, looks like a waste of money; while the ordinary management in which the planning is mainly done by the workmen themselves, with the help of one or two foremen, seems simple and economical in the extreme.

The writer, however, while still a young man, had all lingering doubt as to the value of a drafting room dispelled by seeing the chief engineer, the foreman of the machine shop, the foreman of the foundry, and one or two workmen, in one of our large and successful engineering establishments of the old school, stand over the cylinder of an engine which was being built, with chalk and dividers, and discuss for more than an hour the proper size and location of the studs for fastening on the cylinder head. This was simplicity, but not economy. About the same time he became thoroughly convinced of the necessity and economy of a planning department with time study, and with written instruction cards and returns. He saw over and over again a workman shut down his machine and hunt up the foreman to inquire, perhaps, what work to put into his machine next, and then chase around the shop to find it or to have a special tool or template looked up or made. He saw workmen carefully nursing their jobs by the hour and doing next to nothing to avoid making a record, and he was even more forcibly convinced of the necessity for a change while he was still working as a machinist by being ordered by the other men to slow down to half speed under penalty of being thrown over the fence.

No one now doubts the economy of the drafting room, and the writer predicts that in a very few years from now no one will doubt the economy and necessity of the study of unit times and of the planning department.

Another point of analogy between modern engineering and modern management lies in the fact that modern engineering proceeds with comparative certainty to the design and construction of a machine or structure of the maximum efficiency with the minimum weight and cost of materials, while the old style engineering at best only approximated these results and then only after a series of breakdowns, involving the practical reconstruction of the machine and the lapse of a long period of time. The ordinary system of management, owing to the lack of exact information and precise methods, can only approximate to the desired standard of high wages accompanied by low labor cost and then only slowly, with marked irregularity in results, with continued opposition, and, in many cases, with danger from strikes. Modern management, on the other hand, proceeds slowly at first, but with directness and precision, step by step, and, after the first few object lessons, almost without opposition on the part of the men, to high wages and low labor cost; and as is of great importance, it assigns wages to the men which are uniformly fair. They are not demoralized, and their sense of justice offended by receiving wages which are sometimes too low and at other times entirely too high.

One of the marked advantages of scientific management lies in its freedom from strikes. The writer has never been opposed by a strike, although he has been engaged for a great part of his time since 1883 in introducing this type of management in different parts of the country and in a great variety of industries. The only case of which the writer can think in which a strike under this system might be unavoidable would be that in which most of the employees were members of a labor union, and of a union whose rules were so inflexible and whose members were so stubborn that they were unwilling to try any other system, even though it assured them larger wages than their own. The writer has seen, however, several times after the introduction of this system, the members of labor unions who were working under it leave the union in large numbers because they found that they could do better under the operation of the system than under the laws of the union.

There is no question that the average individual accomplishes the most when he either gives himself, or some one else assigns him, a definite task, namely, a given amount of work which he must do within a given time; and the more elementary the mind and character of the individual the more necessary does it become that each task shall extend over a short period of time only. No school teacher would think of telling children in a general way to study a certain book or subject. It is practically universal to assign each day a definite lesson beginning on one specified page and line and ending on another; and the best progress is made when the conditions are such that a definite study hour or period can be assigned in. which the lesson must be learned. Most of us remain, through a great part of our lives, in this respect, grown-up children, and do our best only under pressure of a task of comparatively short duration. Another and perhaps equally great advantage of assigning a daily task as against ordinary piece work lies in the fact that the success of a good workman or the failure of a poor one is thereby daily and prominently called to the attention of the management. Many a poor workman might be willing to go along in a slipshod way under ordinary piece work, careless as to whether he fell off a little in his output or not. Very few of them, however, would be willing to record a daily failure to accomplish their task even if they were allowed to do so by their foreman; and also since on ordinary piece work the price alone is specified without limiting the time which the job is to take, a quite large falling off in output can in many cases occur without coming to the attention of the management at all. It is for these reasons that the writer has above indicated "a large daily task" for each man as the first of four principles which should be included in the best type of management.

It is evident, however, that it is useless to assign a task unless at the same time adequate measures are taken to enforce its accomplishment. As Artemus Ward says, "I can call the spirits from the windy deep, but damn 'em they won't come!" It is to compel the completion of the daily task then that two of the other principles are required, namely, "high pay for success" and "loss in case of failure." The advantage of Mr. H. L. Gantt's system of "task work with a bonus," and the writer's "differential rate piece work" over the other systems lies in the fact that with each of these the men automatically and daily receive either an extra reward in case of complete success, or a distinct loss in case they fall off even a little.

The four principles above referred to can be successfully applied either under day work, piece work, task work with a bonus, or differential rate piece work, and each of these systems has its own especial conditions under which it is to be preferred to either of the other three. In no case, however, should an attempt

43

be made to apply these principles unless accurate and thorough time study has previously been made of every item entering into the day's task.

They should be applied under day work only when a number of miscellaneous jobs have to be done day after day, none of which can occupy the entire time of a man throughout the whole of a day and when the time required to do each of these small jobs is likely to vary somewhat each day. In this case a number of these jobs can be grouped into a daily task which should be assigned, if practicable, to one man, possibly even to two or three, but rarely to a gang of men of any size. To illustrate: In a small boiler house in which there is no storage room for coal, the work of wheeling the coal to the fireman, wheeling out the ashes, helping clean fires and keeping the boiler room and the outside of the boilers clean can be made into the daily task for a man, and if these items do not sum up into a full day's work, on the average, other duties can be added until a proper task is assured. Or, the various details of sweeping, cleaning, and keeping a certain section of a shop floor windows, machines, etc., in order can be united to form a task. Or, in a small factory which turns out a uniform product and in uniform quantities day after day, supplying raw materials to certain parts of the factory and removing finished product from others may be coupled with other definite duties to form a task. The task should call for a large day's work, and the man should be paid more than the usual day's pay so that the position will be sought for by first-class, ambitious men. Clerical work can very properly be done by the task in this way, although when there is enough of it, piece work at so much per entry is to be preferred.

In all cases a clear cut, definite inspection of the task is desirable at least once a day and sometimes twice. When a shop is not running at night, a good time for this inspection is at seven o'clock in the morning, for instance. The inspector should daily sign a printed card, stating that he has inspected the work done by — —, and enumerating the various items of the task. The card should state that the workman has satisfactorily performed his task, "except the following items," which should be enumerated in detail.

When men are working on task work by the day they should be made to start to work at the regular starting hour. They should, however, have no regular time for leaving. As soon as the task is finished they should be allowed to go home; and, on the other hand, they should be made to stay at work until their task is done, even if it lasts into the night, no deduction being made for shorter hours nor extra pay allowed for overtime. It is both inhuman and unwise to ask a man, working on task work, to stay in the shop after his task is finished "to maintain the discipline of the shop," as is frequently done. It only tends to make men eye servants.

An amusing instance of the value of task work with freedom to leave when the task is done was given the writer by his friend, Mr. Chas. D. Rogers, for many years superintendent of the American Screw Works, of Providence, R. I., one of the greatest mechanical geniuses and most resourceful managers that this country has produced, but a man who, owing to his great modesty, has never been fully appreciated outside of those who know him well. Mr. Rogers tried several modifications of day and piece work in an unsuccessful endeavor to get the children who were engaged in sorting over the very small screws to do a fair day's work. He finally met with great success by assigning to each child a fair day's task and allowing him to go home and play as soon as his task was done. Each child's playtime was his own and highly prized while the greater part of his wages went to his parents.

Piece work embodying the task idea can be used to advantage when there is enough work of the same general character to keep a number of men busy regularly; such work, for instance, as the Bethlehem yard labor previously described, or the work of

45

bicycle ball inspection referred to later on. In piece work of this class the task idea should always be maintained by keeping it clearly before each man that his average daily earnings must amount to a given high sum (as in the case of the Bethlehem laborers, $1.85 per day), and that failure to average this amount will surely result in his being laid off. It must be remembered that on plain piece work the less competent workmen will always bring what influence and pressure they can to cause the best men to slow down towards their level and that the task idea is needed to counteract this influence. Where the labor market is large enough to secure in a reasonable time enough strictly first-class men, the piece work rates should be fixed on such a basis that only a first-class man working at his best can earn the average amount called for. This figure should be, in the case of first-class men as stated above, from 30 per cent to 100 per cent beyond the wages usually paid. The task idea is emphasized with this style of piece work by two things—the high wages and the laying off, after a reasonable trial, of incompetent men; and for the success of the system, the number of men employed on practically the same class of work should be large enough for the workmen quite often to have the object lesson of seeing men laid off for failing to earn high wages and others substituted in their places.

There are comparatively few machine shops, or even manufacturing establishments, in which the work is so uniform in its nature as to employ enough men on the same grade of work and in sufficiently close contact to one another to render piece work preferable to the other systems. In the great majority of cases the work is so miscellaneous in its nature as to call for the employment of workmen varying greatly in their natural ability and attainments, all the way, for instance, from the ordinary laborer, through the trained laborer, helper, rough machinist, fitter, machine hand, to the highly skilled special or all-round mechanic. And while in a large establishment there may be often enough men of the same grade to warrant the

46

adoption of piece work with the task idea, yet, even in this case, they are generally so scattered in different parts of the shop that laying off one of their number for incompetence does not reach the others with sufficient force to impress them with the necessity of keeping up with their task.

It is evident then that, in the great majority of cases, the four leading principles in management can be best applied through either task work with a bonus or the differential piece rate in spite of the slight additional clerical work and the increased difficulty in planning ahead incident to these systems of paying wages. Three of the principles of management given above, namely, (a) a large daily task, (b) high pay for success, and (c) loss in case of failure form the very essence of both of these systems and act as a daily stimulant for the men. The fourth principle of management is a necessary preliminary, since without having first thoroughly standardized all of the conditions surrounding work, neither of these two plans can be successfully applied.

In many cases the greatest good resulting from the application of these systems of paying wages is the indirect gain which comes from the enforced standardization of all details and conditions, large and small, surrounding the work. All of the ordinary systems can be and are almost always applied without adopting and maintaining thorough shop standards. But the task idea can not be carried out without them.

The differential rate piece work is rather simpler in its application than task work with bonus and is the more forceful of the two. It should be used wherever it is practicable, but in no case until after all the accompanying conditions have been perfected and completely standardized and a thorough time study has been made of all of the elements of the work. This system is particularly useful where the same kind of work is repeated day after day, and also whenever the maximum possible output is desired, which is almost always the case in the operation of expensive machinery or of a plant occupying valuable ground or a large building. It is more forceful than task work with a bonus because it not only pulls the man up from the top but pushes him equally hard from the bottom. Both of these systems give the workman a large extra reward when he accomplishes his full task within the given time. With the differential rate, if for any reason he fails to do his full task, he not only loses the large extra premium which is paid for complete success, but in addition he suffers the direct loss of the piece price for each piece by which he falls short. Failure under the task with a bonus system involves a corresponding loss of the extra premium or bonus, but the workman, since he is paid a given price per hour, receives his ordinary day's pay in case of failure and suffers no additional loss beyond that of the extra premium whether he may have fallen short of the task to the extent of one piece or a dozen.

In principle, these two systems appear to be almost identical, yet this small difference, the slightly milder nature of task work with a bonus, is sufficient to render it much more flexible and therefore applicable to a large number of cases in which the differential rate system cannot be used. Task work with a bonus was invented by Mr. H. L. Gantt, while he was assisting the writer in organizing the Bethlehem Steel Company. The possibilities of his system were immediately recognized by all of the leading men engaged on the work, and long before it would have been practicable to use the differential rate, work was started under this plan. It was successful from the start, and steadily grew in volume and in favor, and today is more extensively used than ever before.

Mr. Gantt's system is especially useful during the difficult and delicate period of transition from the slow pace of ordinary day work to the high speed which is the leading characteristic of good management. During this period of transition in the past, a time was always reached when a sudden long leap was taken from improved day work to some form of piece work; and in making this jump many good men inevitably fell and were lost from the procession. Mr. Gantt's system bridges over this difficult stretch and enables the workman to go smoothly and with gradually accelerated speed from the slower pace of improved day work to the high speed of the new system.

It does not appear that Mr. Gantt has recognized the full advantages to be derived through the proper application of his system during this period of transition, at any rate he has failed to point them out in his papers and to call the attention to the best method of applying his plan in such cases.

No workman can be expected to do a piece of work the first time as fast as he will later. It should also be recognized that it takes a certain time for men who have worked at the ordinary slow rate of speed to change to high speed. Mr. Gantt's plan can be adapted to meet both of these conditions by allowing the workman to take a longer time to do the job at first and yet earn his bonus; and later compelling him to finish the job in the quickest time in order to get the premium. In all cases it is of the utmost importance that each instruction card should state the quickest time in which the workman will ultimately be called upon to do the work. There will then be no temptation for the man to soldier since he will see that the management know accurately how fast the work can be done.

There is also a large class of work in addition to that of the period of transition to which task work with a bonus is especially adapted. The higher pressure of the differential rate is the stimulant required by the workman to maintain a high rate of speed and secure high wages while he has the steady swing that belongs to work which is repeated over and over again. When, however, the work is of such variety that each day presents an entirely new task, the pressure of the differential rate is some times too severe. The chances of failing to quite reach the task are greater in this class of work than in routine work; and in many such cases it is better, owing to the increased difficulties, that the workman should feel sure at least of his regular day's rate, which is secured him by Mr. Gantt's system in case he falls short of the full task. There is still another case of quite frequent occurrence in which the flexibility of Mr. Gantt's plan makes it the most desirable. In many establishments, particularly those doing an engineering business of considerable variety or engaged in constructing and erecting miscellaneous machinery, it is necessary to employ continuously a number of especially skilful and high-priced mechanics. The particular work for which these men are wanted comes, however, in many cases, at irregular intervals, and there are frequently quite long waits between their especial jobs. During such periods these men must be provided with work which is ordinarily done by less efficient, lower priced men, and if a proper piece price has been fixed on this work it would naturally be a price suited to the less skilful men, and therefore too low for the men in question. The alternative is presented of trying to compel these especially skilled men to work for a lower price than they should receive, or of fixing a special higher piece price for the work. Fixing two prices for the same piece of work, one for the man who usually does it and a higher price for the higher grade man, always causes the greatest feeling of injustice and dissatisfaction in the man who is discriminated against. With Mr. Gantt's plan the less skilledworkman would recognize the justice of paying his more experienced companion regularly a higher rate of wages by the day, yet when they were both working on the same kind of work each man would receive the same extra bonus for doing the full day's task. Thus, with Mr. Gantt's system, the total day's pay of the higher classed man would be greater than that of the less skilled man, even when on the same work, and the latter would not begrudge it to him. We may say that the difference is one of sentiment, yet sentiment plays an important part in all of our lives; and sentiment is particularly strong in the workman when he believes a direct injustice is being done him.

Mr. James M. Dodge, the distinguished Past President of The American Society of Mechanical Engineers, has invented an ingenious system of piece work which is adapted to meet this very case, and which has especial advantages not possessed by any of the other plans.

It is clear, then, that in carrying out the task idea after the required knowledge has been obtained through a study of unit times, each of the four systems, (a) day work, (b) straight piece work, (c) task work with a bonus, and (d) differential piece work, has its especial field of usefulness, and that in every large establishment doing a variety of work all four of these plans can and should be used at the same time. Three of these systems were in use at the Bethlehem Steel Company when the writer left there, and the fourth would have soon been started if he had remained.

Before leaving this part of the book which has been devoted to pointing out the value of. the daily task in management, it would seem desirable to give an illustration of the value of the differential rate piece work and also of the desirability of making each task as simple and short as practicable.

The writer quotes as follows from a paper entitled "A Piece Rate System," read by him before The American Society of Mechanical Engineers in 1895:

"The first case in which a differential rate was applied during the year 1884, furnishes a good illustration of what can be accomplished by it. A standard steel forging, many thousands of which are used each year, had for several years been turned at the rate of from four to five per day under the ordinary system of piece work, 50 cents per piece being the price paid for the work. After analyzing the job, and determining the shortest time required to do each of the elementary operations of which it was composed, and then summing up the total, the writer became convinced that it was possible to turn ten pieces a day. To finish

51

the forgings at this rate, however, the machinists were obliged to work at their maximum pace from morning to night, and the lathes were run as fast as the tools would allow, and under a heavy feed. Ordinary tempered tools 1 inch by 1 1/2 inch, made of carbon tool steel, were used for this work.

"It will be appreciated that this was a big day's work, both for men and machines, when it is understood that it involved removing, with a single 16-inch lathe, having two saddles, an average of more than 800 lbs of steel chips in ten hours. In place of the 50 cent rate, that they had been paid before, the men were given 35 cents per piece when they turned them at the speed of 10 per day; and when they produced less than ten they received only 25 cents per piece.

"It took considerable trouble to induce the men to turn at this high speed, since they did not at first fully appreciate that it was the intention of the firm to allow them to earn permanently at the rate of $3.50 per day. But from the day they first turned ten pieces to the present time, a period of more than ten years, the men who understood their work have scarcely failed a single day to turn at this rate. Throughout that time until the beginning of the recent fall in the scale of wages throughout the country, the rate was not cut.

"During this whole period, the competitors of the company never succeeded in averaging over half of this production per lathe, although they knew and even saw what was being done at Midvale. They, however, did not allow their men to earn from over $2.00 to $2.50 per day, and so never even approached the maximum output.

"The following table will show the economy of paying high wages under the differential rate in doing the above job:

"COST OF PRODUCTION PER LATHE PER DAY

ORDINARY SYSTEM OF PIECE WORK—Man's wages $2.50

Machine cost 3.37 Total cost per day 5.87 5 pieces produced; Cost per piece $1.17

DIFFERENTIAL RATE SYSTEM—Man's wages $3.50 Machine cost 3.37 Total cost per day 6.87 10 pieces produced; Cost per piece $0.69

"The above result was mostly though not entirely due to the differential rate. The superior system of managing all of the small details of the shop counted for considerable."

The exceedingly dull times that began in July, 1893, and were accompanied by a great fall in prices, rendered it necessary to lower the wages of machinists throughout the country. The wages of the men in A. the Midvale Steel Works were reduced at this time, and the change was accepted by them as fair and just.

Throughout the works, however, the principle of the differential rate was maintained, and was, and is still, fully appreciated by both the management and men. Through some error at the time of the general reduction of wages in 1893, the differential rate on the particular job above referred to was removed, and a straight piece work rate of 25 cents per piece was substituted for it. The result of abandoning the differential proved to be the best possible demonstration of its value. Under straight piece work, the output immediately fell to between six and eight pieces per day, and remained at this figure for several years, although under the differential rate it had held throughout a long term of years steadily at ten per day.

When work is to be repeated many times, the time study should be minute and exact. Each job should be carefully subdivided into its elementary operations, and each of these unit times should receive the most thorough time study. In fixing the times for the tasks, and the piece work rates on jobs of this class, the job should be subdivided into a number of divisions, and a separate time and price assigned to each division rather than to

53

assign a single time and price for the whole job. This should be done for several reasons, the most important of which is that the average workman, in order to maintain a rapid pace, should be given the opportunity of measuring his performance against the task set him at frequent intervals. Many men are incapable of looking very far ahead, but if they see a definite opportunity of earning so many cents by working hard for so many minutes, they will avail themselves of it.

As an illustration, the steel tires used on car wheels and locomotives were originally turned in the Midvale Steel Works on piece work, a single piece-work rate being paid for all of the work which could be done on a tire at a single setting. A fixed price was paid for this work, whether there was much or little metal to be removed, and on the average this price was fair to the men. The apparent advantage of fixing a fair average rate was, that it made rate-fixing exceedingly simple, and saved clerk work in the time, cost and record keeping.

A careful time study, however, convinced the writer that for the reasons given above most of the men failed to do their best. In place of the single rate and time for all of the work done at a setting, the writer subdivided tire-turning into a number of short operations, and fixed a proper time and price, varying for each small job, according to the amount of metal to be removed, and the hardness and diameter of the tire. The effect of this subdivision was to increase the output, with the same men, methods, and machines, at least thirty-three per cent.

As an illustration of the minuteness of this subdivision, an instruction card similar to the one used is reproduced in Figure 1 on the next page. (This card was about 7 inches long by 4 inches wide.)

[Transcriber's note — Figure 1 not shown]

The cost of the additional clerk work involved in this change

54

was so insignificant that it practically did not affect the problem. This principle of short tasks in tire turning was introduced by the writer in the Midvale Steel Works in 1883 and is still in full use there, having survived the test of over twenty years' trial with a change of management.

In another establishment a differential rate was applied to tire turning, with operations subdivided in this way, by adding fifteen per cent to the pay of each tire turner whenever his daily or weekly piece work earnings passed a given figure.

Another illustration of the application of this principle of measuring a man's performance against a given task at frequent intervals to an entirely different line of work may be of interest. For this purpose the writer chooses the manufacture of bicycle balls in the works of the Symonds Rolling Machine Company, in Fitchburg, Mass. All of the work done in this factory was subjected to an accurate time study, and then was changed from day to piece work, through the assistance of functional foreman ship, etc. The particular operation to be described however, is that of inspecting bicycle balls before they were finally boxed for shipment. Many millions of these balls were inspected annually. When the writer undertook to systematize this work, the factory had been running for eight or ten years on ordinary day work, so that the various employees were "old hands," and skilled at their jobs. The work of inspection was done entirely by girls—about one hundred and twenty being employed at it—all on day work.

This work consisted briefly in placing a row of small polished steel balls on the back of the left hand, in the crease between two of the fingers pressed together, and while they were rolled over and over, with the aid of a magnet held in the right hand, they were minutely examined in a strong light, and the defective balls picked out and thrown into especial boxes. Four kinds of defects were looked for—dented, soft, scratched, and fire cracked—and they were mostly 50 minute as to be invisible to an eye not especially trained to this work. It required the closest attention

55

and concentration. The girls had worked on day work for years, ten and one-half hours per day, with a Saturday half-holiday.

The first move before in any way stimulating them toward a larger output was to insure against a falling off in quality. This was accomplished through over-inspection. Four of the most trustworthy girls were given each a lot of balls which had been examined the day before by one of the regular inspectors. The number identifying the lot having been changed by the foreman so that none of the over-inspectors knew whose work they were examining. In addition, one of the lots inspected by the four over-inspectors was examined on the following day by the chief inspector, selected on account of her accuracy and integrity.

An effective expedient was adopted for checking the honesty and accuracy of the over-inspection. Every two or three days a lot of balls was especially prepared by the foreman, who counted out a definite number of perfect balls, and added a recorded number of defective balls of each kind. The inspectors had no means of distinguishing this lot from the regular commercial lots. And in this way all temptation to slight their work or make false returns was removed.

After insuring in this way against deterioration in quality, effective means were at once adopted to increase the output. Improved day work was substituted for the old slipshod method. An accurate daily record, both as to quantity and quality, was kept for each inspector. In a comparatively short time this enabled the foreman to stir the ambition of all the inspectors by increasing the wages of those who turned out a large quantity and good quality, at the same time lowering the pay of those who fell short, and discharging others who proved to be incorrigibly slow or careless. An accurate time study was made through the use of a stop watch and record blanks, to determine how fast each kind of inspection should be done. This showed that the girls spent a considerable part of their time in partial idleness, talking and half working, or in actually doing nothing.

Talking while at work was stopped by seating them far apart. The hours of work were shortened from 10 1/2 per day, first to 9 1/2, and later to 8 1/2; a Saturday half holiday being given them even with the shorter hours. Two recesses of ten minutes each were given them, in the middle of the morning and afternoon, during which they were expected to leave their seats, and were allowed to talk.

The shorter hours and improved conditions made it possible for the girls to really work steadily, instead of pretending to do so. Piece work was then introduced, a differential rate being paid, not for an increase in output, but for greater accuracy in the inspection; the lots inspected by the over-inspectors forming the basis for the payment of the differential. The work of each girl was measured every hour, and they were all informed whether they were keeping up with their tasks, or how far they had fallen short and an assistant was sent by the foreman to encourage those who were falling behind, and help them to catch up.

The principle of measuring the performance of each workman against a standard at frequent intervals, of keeping them informed as to their progress, and of sending an assistant to help those who were falling down, was carried out throughout the works, and proved to be most useful.

The final results of the improved system in the inspecting department were as follows:

(a) Thirty-five girls did the work formerly done by one hundred and twenty.

(b) The girls averaged from $6.50 to $9.00 per week instead of $3.50 to $4.50, as formerly.

(c) They worked only 8 1/2 hours per day, with Saturday a half-holiday, while they had formerly worked 10 1/2 hours per day.

57

(d) An accurate comparison of the balls which were inspected under the old system of day work with those done under piece work, with over-inspection, showed that, in spite of the large increase in output per girl, there were 58 per cent more defective balls left in the product as sold under day work than under piece work. In other words, the accuracy of inspection under piece work was one-third greater than that under day work.

That thirty-five girls were able to do the work which formerly required about one hundred and twenty is due, not only to the improvement in the work of each girl, owing to better methods, but to the weeding out of the lazy and unpromising candidates, and the substitution of more ambitious individuals.

A more interesting illustration of the effect of the improved conditions and treatment is shown in the following comparison. Records were kept of the work of ten girls, all "old hands," and good inspectors, and the improvement made by these skilled hands is undoubtedly entirely due to better management. All of these girls throughout the period of comparison were engaged on the same kind of work, viz.: inspecting bicycle balls, three-sixteenths of an inch in diameter.

The work of organization began in March, and although the records for the first three months were not entirely clear, the increased output due to better day work amounted undoubtedly to about 33 per cent. The increase per day from June on day work, to July on piece work, the hours each month being 10 1/2 per day, was 37 per cent. This increase was due to the introduction of piece work. The increase per day from July to August (the length of working days in July being 10 1/2 hours, and in August 9 1/2 hours, both months piece work) was 33 per cent.

The increase from August to September (the length of working day in August being 9 1/2 hours, and in September 8 1/2 hours) was 0.08 per cent This means that the girls did practically the same amount of work per day in September, in 8 1/2 hours, that they did in August in 9 1/2 hours.

To summarize: the same ten girls did on an average each day in September, on piece work, when only working 8 1/2 hours per day, 2.42 times as much, or nearly two and one-half times as much, in a day (not per hour, the increase per hour was of course much greater) as they had done when working on day work in March with a working day of 10 1/2 hours. They earned $6.50 to $9.00 per week on piece work, while they had only earned $3.50 to $4.50 on day work. The accuracy of inspection under piece work was one-third greater than under day work.

The time study for this work was done by my friend, Sanford E. Thompson, C. E. who also had the actual management of the girls throughout the period of transition. At this time Mr. H. L. Gantt was general superintendent of the company, and the work of systematizing was under the general direction of the writer. It is, of course, evident that the nature of the organizations required to manage different types of business must vary to an enormous extent, from the simple tonnage works (with its uniform product, which is best managed by a single strong man who carries all of the details in his head and who, with a few comparatively cheap assistants, pushes the enterprise through to success) to the large machine works, doing a miscellaneous business, with its intricate organization, in which the work of any one man necessarily counts for but little.

It is this great difference in the type of the organization required that so frequently renders managers who have been eminently successful in one line utter failures when they undertake the direction of works of a different kind. This is particularly true of men successful in tonnage work who are placed in charge of shops involving much greater detail.

In selecting an organization for illustration, it would seem best to choose one of the most elaborate. The manner in which this can be simplified to suit a less intricate case will readily suggest itself to any one interested in the subject. One of the most difficult works to organize is that of a large engineering establishment building miscellaneous machinery, and the writer has therefore chosen this for description.

Practically all of the shops of this class are organized upon what may be called the military plan. The orders from the general are transmitted through the colonels, majors, captains, lieutenants and noncommissioned officers to the men. In the same way the orders in industrial establishments go from the manager through superintendents, foremen of shops, assistant foremen and gang bosses to the men. In an establishment of this kind the duties of the foremen, gang bosses, etc., are so varied, and call for an amount of special information coupled with such a variety of natural ability, that only men of unusual qualities to start with, and who have had years of special training, can perform them in a satisfactory manner. It is because of the difficulty—almost the impossibility of getting suitable foremen and gang bosses, more than for any other reason, that we so seldom hear of a miscellaneous machine works starting in on a large scale and meeting with much, if any, success for the first few years. This difficulty is not fully realized by the managers of the old well established companies, since their superintendents and assistants have grown up with the business, and have been gradually worked into and fitted for their especial duties through years of training and the process of natural selection. Even in these establishments, however, this difficulty has impressed itself upon the managers so forcibly that most of them have of late years spent thousands of dollars in re-grouping their machine tools for the purpose of making their foremanship more effective. The planers have been placed in one group, slotters in another, lathes in another, etc., so as to demand a smaller range of experience and less diversity of knowledge from their respective foremen.

For an establishment, then, of this kind, starting up on a large scale, it may be said to be an impossibility to get suitable superintendents and foremen.

The writer found this difficulty at first to be an almost insurmountable obstacle to his work in organizing manufacturing establishments; and after years of experience, overcoming the opposition of the heads of departments and the foremen and gang bosses, and training them to their new duties, still remains the greatest problem in organization. The writer has had comparatively little trouble in inducing workmen to change their ways and to increase their speed, providing the proper object lessons are presented to them, and time enough is allowed for these to produce their effect. It is rarely the case, however, that superintendents and foremen can find any reasons for changing their methods, which, as far as they can see, have been successful. And having, as a rule, obtained their positions owing to their unusual force of character, and being accustomed daily to rule other men, their opposition is generally effective.

In the writer's experience, almost all shops are under-officered. Invariably the number of leading men employed is not sufficient to do the work economically. Under the military type of organization, the foreman is held responsible for the successful running of the entire shop, and when we measure his duties by the standard of the four leading principles of management above referred to, it becomes apparent that in his case these conditions are as far as possible from being fulfilled. His duties may be briefly enumerated in the following way. He must lay out the work for the whole shop, see that each piece of work goes in the proper order to the right machine, and that the man at the machine knows just what is to be done and how he is to do it. He must see that the work is not slighted, and that it is done fast, and all the while he must look ahead a month or so, either to provide more men to do the work or more work for the men to do. He must constantly discipline the men and readjust their wages, and in addition to this must fix piece work prices and supervise the timekeeping.

The first of the four leading principles in management calls for a clearly defined and circumscribed task. Evidently the foreman's duties are in no way clearly circumscribed. It is left each day entirely to his judgment what small part of the mass of duties before him it is most important for him to attend to, and he staggers along under this fraction of the work for which he is responsible, leaving the balance to be done in many cases as the gang bosses and workmen see fit. The second principle calls for such conditions that the daily task can always be accomplished. The conditions in his case are always such that it is impossible for him to do it all, and he never even makes pretence of fulfilling his entire task. The third and fourth principles call for high pay in case the task is successfully done, and low pay in case of failure. The failure to realize the first two conditions, however, renders the application of the last two out of the question.

The foreman usually endeavors to lighten his burdens by delegating his duties to the various assistant foremen or gang bosses in charge of lathes, planers, milling machines, vise work, etc. Each of these men is then called upon to perform duties of almost as great variety as those of the foreman himself. The difficulty in obtaining in one man the variety of special information and the different mental and moral qualities necessary to perform all of the duties demanded of those men has been clearly summarized in the following list of the nine qualities which go to make up a well rounded man:

Brains.

Education.

Special or technical knowledge; manual dexterity or strength.

Tact.

Energy.

Grit.

Honesty.

Judgment or common sense and

Good health.

Plenty of men who possess only three of the above qualities can be hired at any time for laborers' wages. Add four of these qualities together and you get a higher priced man. The man combining five of these qualities begins to be hard to find, and those with six, seven, and eight are almost impossible to get. Having this fact in mind, let us go over the duties which a gang boss in charge, say, of lathes or planers, is called upon to perform, and note the knowledge and qualities which they call for. First. He must be a good machinist—and this alone calls for years of special training, and limits the choice to a comparatively small class of men.

Second. He must be able to read drawings readily, and have sufficient imagination to see the work in its finished state clearly before him. This calls for at least a certain amount of brains and education.

Third. He must plan ahead and see that the right jigs, clamps, and appliances, as well as proper cutting tools, are on hand, and are used to set the work correctly in the machine and cut the metal at the right speed and feed. This calls for the ability to concentrate the mind upon a multitude of small details, and take pains with little, uninteresting things.

Fourth. He must see that each man keeps his machine clean and in good order. This calls for the example of a man who is naturally neat and orderly himself.

Fifth. He must see that each man turns out work of the proper quality. This calls for the conservative judgment and the honesty which are the qualities of a good inspector.

Sixth. He must see that the men under him work steadily and fast. To accomplish this he should himself be a hustler, a man of energy, ready to pitch in and infuse life into his men by working faster than they do, and this quality is rarely combined with the painstaking care, the neatness and the conservative judgment demanded as the third, fourth, and fifth requirements of a gang boss.

Seventh. He must constantly look ahead over the whole field of work and see that the parts go to the machines in their proper sequence, and that the right job gets to each machine.

Eighth. He must, at least in a general way, supervise the timekeeping and fix piece work rates. Both the seventh and eighth duties call for a certain amount of clerical work and ability, and this class of work is almost always repugnant to the man suited to active executive work, and difficult for him to do; and the rate-fixing alone requires the whole time and careful study of a man especially suited to its minute detail.

Ninth. He must discipline the men under him, and readjust their wages; and these duties call for judgment, tact, and judicial fairness.

It is evident, then, that the duties which the ordinary gang boss is called upon to perform would demand of him a large proportion of the nine attributes mentioned above; and if such a man could be found he should be made manager or superintendent of a works instead of gang boss. However, bearing in mind the fact that plenty of men can be had who combine four or five of these attributes, it becomes evident that the work of management should be so subdivided that the various positions can be filled by men of this caliber, and a great part of the art of management undoubtedly lies in planning the

64

work in this way. This can, in the judgment of the writer, be best accomplished by abandoning the military type of organization and introducing two broad and sweeping changes in the art of management:

(a) As far as possible the workmen, as well as the gang bosses and foremen, should be entirely relieved of the work of planning, and of all work which is more or less clerical in its nature. All possible brain work should be removed from the shop and centered in the planning or laying-out department, leaving for the foremen and gang bosses work strictly executive in its nature. Their duties should be to see that the operations planned and directed from the planning room are promptly carried out in the shop. Their time should be spent with the men, teaching them to think ahead, and leading and instructing them in their work.

(b) Throughout the whole field of management the military type of organization should be abandoned, and what may be called the' "functional type" substituted in its place. "Functional management" consists in so dividing the work of management that each man from the assistant superintendent down shall have as few functions as possible to perform. If practicable the work of each man in the management should be confined to the performance of a single leading function. Under the ordinary or military type, the workmen are divided into groups. The men in each group receive their orders from one man only, the foreman or gang boss of that group. This man is the single agent through which the various functions of the management are brought into contact with the men. Certainly the most marked outward characteristic of functional management lies in the fact that each workman, instead of coming in direct contact with the management at one point only, namely, through his gang boss, receives his daily orders and help directly from eight different bosses, each of whom performs his own particular function. Four of these bosses are in the planning room and of these three send their orders to and receive their returns from the men, usually in writing. Four others are in the shop and personally help the men in their work, each boss helping in his own particular `line or function only. Some of these bosses come in contact with each man only once or twice a day and then for a few minutes perhaps, while others are with the men all the time, and help each man frequently. The functions of one or two of these bosses require them to come in contact with each workman for so short a time each day that they can perform their particular duties perhaps for all of the men in the shop, and in their line they manage the entire shop. Other bosses are called upon to help their men so much and so often that each boss can perform his function for but a few men, and in this particular line a number of bosses are required, all performing the same function but each having his particular group of men to help. Thus the grouping of the men in the shop is entirely changed, each workman belonging to eight different groups according to the particular functional boss whom he happens to be working under at the moment.

The following is a brief description of the duties of the four types of executive functional bosses which the writer has found it profitable to use in the active work of the shop: (1) gang bosses, (2) speed bosses, (3) inspectors, and (4) repair bosses.

The gang boss has charge of the preparation of all work up to the time that the piece is set in the machine. It is his duty to see that every man under him has at all times at least one piece of work ahead at his machine, with all the jigs, templates, drawings, driving mechanism, sling chains, etc., ready to go into his machine as soon as the piece he is actually working on is done. The gang boss must show his men how to set their work in their machines in the quickest time, and see that they do it. He is responsible for the work being accurately and quickly set, and should be not only able but willing to pitch in himself and show the men how to set the work in record time.

The speed boss must see that the proper cutting tools are used for each piece of work, that the work is properly driven, that the cuts are started in the right part of the piece, and that the best speeds and feeds and depth of cut are used. His work begins only after the piece is in the lathe or planer, and ends when the actual machining ends. The speed boss must not only advise his men how best to do this work, but he must see that they do it in the quickest time, and that they use the speeds and feeds and depth of cut as directed on the instruction card In many cases he is called upon to demonstrate that the work can be done in the specified time by doing it himself in the presence of his men.

The inspector is responsible for the quality of the work, and both the workmen and speed bosses must see that the work is all finished to suit him. This man can, of course, do his work best if he is a master of the art of finishing work both well and quickly.

The repair boss sees that each workman keeps his machine clean, free from rust and scratches, and that he oils and treats it properly, and that all of the standards established for the care and maintenance of the machines and their accessories are rigidly maintained, such as care of belts and shifters, cleanliness of floor around machines, and orderly piling and disposition of work.

The following is an outline of the duties of the four functional bosses who are located in the planning room, and who in their various functions represent the department in its connection with the men. The first three of these send their directions to and receive their returns from the men, mainly in writing. These four representatives of the planning department are, the (1) order of work and route clerk, (2) instruction card clerk, (3) time and cost clerk, and (4) shop disciplinarian.

Order of Work and Route Clerk. After the route clerk in the planning department has laid out the exact route which each piece of work is to travel through the shop from machine to machine in order that it may be finished at the time it is needed for assembling, and the work done in the most economical way, the order of work clerk daily writes lists instructing the workmen and also all of the executive shop bosses as to the exact order in which the work is to be done by each class of machines or men, and these lists constitute the chief means for directing the workmen in this particular function.

Instruction Card Clerks. The "instruction card," as its name indicates, is the chief means employed by the planning department for instructing both the executive bosses and the men in all of the details of their work. It tells them briefly the general and detail drawing to refer to, the piece number and the cost order number to charge the work to, the special jigs, fixtures, or tools to use, where to start each cut, the exact depth of each cut, and how many cuts to take, the speed and feed to be used for each cut, and the time within which each operation must be finished. It also informs them as to the piece rate, the differential rate, or the premium to be paid for completing the task within the specified time (according to the system employed); and further, when necessary, refers them by name to the man who will give them especial directions. This instruction card is filled in by one or more members of the planning department, according to the nature and complication of the instructions, and bears the same relation to the planning room that the drawing does to the drafting room. The man who sends it into the shop and who, in case difficulties are met with in carrying out the instructions, sees that the proper man sweeps these difficulties away, is called the instruction card foreman.

Time and Cost Clerk. This man sends to the men through the "time ticket" all the information they need for recording their time and the cost of the work, and secures proper returns from them. He refers these for entry to the cost and time record clerks in the planning room.

Shop Disciplinarian. In case of insubordination or impudence, repeated failure to do their duty, lateness or unexcused absence, the shop disciplinarian takes the workman or bosses in hand and applies the proper remedy. He sees that a complete record of each man's virtues and defects is kept. This man should also have much to do with readjusting the wages of the workmen. At the very least, he should invariably be consulted before any change is made. One of his important functions should be that of peace-maker.

Thus, under functional foremanship, we see that the work which, under the military type of organization, was done by the single gang boss, is subdivided among eight men: (1) route clerks, (2) instruction card clerks, (3) cost and time clerks, who plan and give directions from the planning room; (4) gang bosses, (5) speed bosses, (6) inspectors, (7) repair bosses, who show the men how to carry out their instructions, and see that the work is done at the proper speed; and (8) the shop disciplinarian, who performs this function for the entire establishment.

The greatest good resulting from this change is that it becomes possible in a comparatively short time to train bosses who can really and fully perform the functions demanded of them, while under the old system it took years to train men who were after all able to thoroughly perform only a portion of their duties. A glance at the nine qualities needed for a well rounded man and then at the duties of these functional foremen will show that each of these men requires but a limited number of the nine qualities in order to successfully fill his position; and that the special knowledge which he must acquire forms only a small part of that needed by the old style gang boss. The writer has seen men taken (some of them from the ranks of the workmen, others from the old style bosses and others from among the graduates of industrial schools, technical schools and colleges) and trained to become efficient functional foremen in from six to eighteen months. Thus it becomes possible with functional foremanship to thoroughly and completely equip even a new company starting on a large scale with competent officers in a reasonable time, which is entirely out of the question under the old system. Another great advantage resulting from functional or divided foremanship is that it becomes entirely practicable to apply the four leading principles of management to the bosses as well as to the workmen. Each foreman can have a task assigned him which is so accurately measured that he will be kept fully occupied and still will daily be able to perform his entire function. This renders it possible to pay him high wages when he is successful by giving him a premium similar to that offered the men and leave him with low pay when he fails.

The full possibilities of functional foremanship, however, will not have been realized until almost all of the machines in the shop are run by men who are of smaller calibre and attainments, and who are therefore cheaper than those required under the old system. The adoption of standard tools, appliances, and methods throughout the shop, the planning done in the planning room and the detailed instructions sent them from this department, added to the direct help received from the four executive bosses, permit the use of comparatively cheap men even on complicated work. Of the men in the machine shop of the Bethlehem Steel Company engaged in running the roughing machines, and who were working under the bonus system when the writer left them, about 95 per cent were handy men trained up from laborers. And on the finishing machines, working on bonus, about 25 per cent were handy men.

To fully understand the importance of the work which was being done by these former laborers, it must be borne in mind that a considerable part of their work was very large and expensive. The forgings which they were engaged in roughing and finishing weighed frequently many tons. Of course they were paid more than laborer's wages, though not as much as skilled machinists. The work in this shop was most miscellaneous in its nature.

Functional foremanship is already in limited use in many of the best managed shops. A number of managers have seen the practical good that arises from allowing two or three men especially trained in their particular lines to deal directly with the men instead of at second hand through the old style gang boss as a mouthpiece. So deep rooted, however, is the conviction that the very foundation of management rests in the military type as represented by the principle that no workman can work under two bosses at the same time, that all of the managers who are making limited use of the functional plan seem to feel it necessary to apologize for or explain away their use of it; as not really in this particular case being a violation of that principle. The writer has never yet found one, except among the works which he had assisted in organizing, who came out squarely and acknowledged that he was using functional foremanship because it was the right principle.

The writer introduced five of the elements of functional foremanship into the management of the small machine shop of the Midvale Steel Company of Philadelphia while he was foreman of that shop in 1882-1883: (1) the instruction card clerk, (2) the time clerk, (3) the inspector, (4) the gang boss, and (5) the shop disciplinarian. Each of these functional foremen dealt directly with the workmen instead of giving their orders through the gang boss. The dealings of the instruction card clerk and time clerk with the workmen were mostly in writing, and the writer himself performed the functions of shop disciplinarian, so that it was not until he introduced the inspector, with orders to go straight to the men instead of to the gang boss, that he appreciated the desirability of functional foremanship as a distinct principle in management. The prepossession in favor of the military type was so strong with the managers and owners of Midvale that it was not until years after functional foremanship was in continual use in this shop that he dared to advocate it to his superior officers as the correct principle.

Until very recently in his organization of works he has found it best to first introduce five or six of the elements of functional foremanship quietly, and get them running smoothly in a shop before calling attention to the principle involved. When the time for this announcement comes, it invariably acts as the proverbial red rag on the bull. It was some years later that the writer subdivided the duties of the "old gang boss" who spent his whole time with the men into the four functions of (1) speed boss, (2) repair boss, (3) inspector, and (4) gang boss, and it is the introduction of these four shop bosses directly helping the men (particularly that of the speed boss) in place of the single old boss, that has produced the greatest improvement in the shop.

When functional foremanship is introduced in a large shop, it is desirable that all of the bosses who are performing the same function should have their own foreman over them; for instance, the speed bosses should have a speed foreman over them, the gang bosses, a head gang boss; the inspectors, a chief inspector, etc., etc. The functions of these over-foremen are twofold. The first part of their work is to teach each of the bosses under them the exact nature of his duties, and at the start, also to nerve and brace them up to the point of insisting that the workmen shall carry out the orders exactly as specified on the instruction cards. This is a difficult task at first, as the workmen have been accustomed for years to do the details of the work to suit themselves, and many of them are intimate friends of the bosses and believe they know quite as much about their business as the latter. The second function of the over-foreman is to smooth out the difficulties which arise between the different types of bosses who in turn directly help the men. The speed boss, for instance, always follows after the gang boss on any particular job in taking charge of the workmen. In this way their respective duties come in contact edgeways, as it were, for a short time, and at the start there is sure to be more or less friction between the two. If two of these bosses meet with a difficulty which they cannot settle, they send for their respective over-foremen, who are

72

usually able to straighten it out. In case the latter are unable to agree on the remedy, the case is referred by them to the assistant superintendent, whose duties, for a certain time at least, may consist largely in arbitrating such difficulties and thus establishing the unwritten code of laws by which the shop is governed. This serves as one example of what is called the "exception principle" in management, which is referred to later.

Before leaving this portion of the subject the writer wishes to call attention to the analogy which functional foremanship bears to the management of a large, up-to-date school. In such a school the children are each day successively taken in hand by one teacher after another who is trained in his particular specialty, and they are in many cases disciplined by a man particularly trained in this function. The old style, one teacher to a class plan is entirely out of date.

The writer has found that better results are attained by placing the planning department in one office, situated, of course, as close to the center of the shop or shops as practicable, rather than by locating its members in different places according to their duties. This department performs more or less the functions of a clearing house. In doing their various duties, its members must exchange information frequently, and since they send their orders to and receive their returns from the men in the shop, principally in writing, simplicity calls for the use, when possible, of a single piece of paper for each job for conveying the instructions of the different members of the planning room to the men and another similar paper for receiving the returns from the men to the department. Writing out these orders and acting promptly on receipt of the returns and recording same requires the members of the department to be close together. The large machine shop of the Bethlehem Steel Company was more than a quarter of a mile long, and this was successfully run from a single planning room situated close to it. The manager, superintendent, and their assistants should, of course, have their offices adjacent to the planning room and, if practicable, the drafting room should be near at hand, thus bringing all of the planning and purely brain work of the establishment close together. The advantages of this concentration were found to be so great at Bethlehem that the general offices of the company, which were formerly located in the business part of the town, about a mile and a half away, were moved into the middle of the works adjacent to the planning room.

The shop, and indeed the whole works, should be managed, not by the manager, superintendent, or foreman, but by the planning department. The daily routine of running the entire works should be carried on by the various functional elements of this department, so that, in theory at least, the works could run smoothly even if the manager, superintendent and their assistants outside the planning room were all to be away for a month at a time.

The following are the leading functions of the planning department:

(a) The complete analysis of all orders for machines or work taken by the company.

(b) Time study for all work done by hand throughout the works, including that done in setting the work in machines, and all bench, vise work and transportation, etc.

(c) Time study for all operations done by the various machines.

(d) The balance of all materials, raw materials, stores and finished parts, and the balance of the work ahead for each class of machines and workmen.

(e) The analysis of all inquiries for new work received in the sales department and promises for time of delivery.

(f) The cost of all items manufactured with complete expense analysis and complete monthly comparative cost and expense exhibits.

(g) The pay department.

(h) The mnemonic symbol system for identification of parts and for charges.

(i) Information bureau.

(j) Standards.

(k) Maintenance of system and plant, and use of the tickler.

(l) Messenger system and post office delivery.

(m) Employment bureau.

(n) Shop disciplinarian.

(o) A mutual accident insurance association.

(p) Rush order department.

(q) Improvement of system or plant.

These several functions may be described more in detail as follows:

(a) THE COMPLETE ANALYSIS OF ALL ORDERS FOR MACHINES OR WORK TAKEN BY THE COMPANY.

This analysis should indicate the designing and drafting required, the machines or parts to be purchased and all data needed by the purchasing agent, and as soon as the necessary drawings and information come from the drafting room the lists of patterns, castings and forgings to be made, together with all instructions for making them, including general and detail drawing, piece number, the mnemonic symbol belonging to each piece (as referred to under (h) below) a complete analysis of the successive operations to be done on each piece, and the exact route which each piece is to travel from place to place in the works.

(b) TIME STUDY FOR ALL WORK DONE BY HAND THROUGHOUT THE WORKS, INCLUDING THAT DONE IN SETTING THE WORK IN MACHINES, AND ALL BENCH AND VISE WORK, AND TRANSPORTATION, ETC.

This information for each particular operation should be obtained by summing up the various unit times of which it consists. To do this, of course, requires the men performing this function to keep continually posted as to the best methods and appliances to use, and also to frequently consult with and receive advice from the executive gang bosses who carry out this work in the shop, and from the man in the department of standards and maintenance of plant (j) beneath. The actual study of unit times, of course, forms the greater part of the work of this section of the planning room.

(c) TIME STUDY FOR ALL OPERATIONS DONE BY THE VARIOUS MACHINES.

This information is best obtained from slide rules, one of which is made for each machine tool or class of machine tools throughout the works; one, for instance, for small lathes of the same type, one for planers of same type, etc. These slide rules show the best way to machine each piece and enable detailed directions to be given the workman as to how many cuts to take, where to start each cut, both for roughing out work and finishing it, the depth of the cut, the best feed and speed, and the exact time required to do each operation.

The information obtained through function (b), together with that obtained through (c) afford the basis for fixing the proper piece rate, differential rate or the bonus to be paid, according to the system employed.

76

(d) THE BALANCE OF ALL MATERIALS, RAW MATERIALS, STORES AND FINISHED PARTS, AND THE NUMBER OF DAYS' WORK AHEAD FOR EACH CLASS OF MACHINES AND WORKMEN.

Returns showing all receipts, as well as the issue of all raw materials, stores, partly finished work, and completed parts and machines, repair parts, etc., daily pass through the balance clerk, and each item of which there have been issues or receipts, or which has been appropriated to the use of a machine about to be manufactured, is daily balanced. Thus the balance clerk can see that the required stocks of materials are kept on hand by notifying at once the purchasing agent or other proper party when the amount on hand falls below the prescribed figure. The balance clerk should also keep a complete running balance of the hours of work ahead for each class of machines and workmen, receiving for this purpose daily from (a), (b), and (c) above statements of the hours of new work entered, and from the inspectors and daily time cards a statement of the work as it is finished. He should keep the manager and sales department posted through daily or weekly condensed reports as to the number of days of work ahead for each department, and thus enable them to obviate either a congestion or scarcity of work.

(e) THE ANALYSIS OF ALL INQUIRIES FOR NEW WORK RECEIVED IN THE SALES DEPARTMENT AND PROMISES AS TO TIME OF DELIVERY. The man or men in the planning room who perform the duties indicated at (a) above should consult with (b) and (c) and obtain from them approximately the time required to do the work inquired for, and from (d) the days of work ahead for the various machines and departments, and inform the sales department as to the probable time required to do the work and the earliest date of delivery.

(f) THE COST OF ALL ITEMS MANUFACTURED, WITH COMPLETE EXPENSE ANALYSIS AND COMPLETE MONTHLY COMPARATIVE COST AND EXPENSE EXHIBITS.

The books of the company should be closed once a month and balanced as completely as they usually are at the end of the year, and the exact cost of each article of merchandise finished during the previous month should be entered on a comparative cost sheet. The expense exhibit should also be a comparative sheet. The cost account should be a completely balanced account, and not a memorandum account as it generally is. All the expenses of the establishment, direct and indirect, including the administration and sales expense, should be charged to the cost of the product which is to be sold.

(g) THE PAY DEPARTMENT.

The pay department should include not only a record of the time and wages and piece work earnings of each man, and his weekly or monthly payment, but the entire supervision of the arrival and departure of the men from the works and the various checks needed to insure against error or cheating. It is desirable that some one of the "exception systems" of time keeping should be used.

(h) THE MNEMONIC SYMBOL SYSTEM FOR IDENTIFICATION OF PARTS AND FOR CHARGES.

Some one of the mnemonic symbol systems should be used instead of numbering the parts or orders for identifying the various articles of manufacture, as well as the operations to be performed on each piece and the various expense charges of the establishment. This becomes a matter of great importance when written directions are sent from the planning room to the men, and the men make their returns in writing. The clerical work and chances for error are thereby greatly diminished.

(i) INFORMATION BUREAU.

The information bureau should include catalogues of drawings (providing the drafting room is close enough to the planning room) as well as all records and reports for the whole establishment. The art of properly indexing information is by no means a simple one, and as far as possible it should be centered in one man.

(j) STANDARDS.

The adoption and maintenance of standard tools, fixtures, and appliances down to the smallest item throughout the works and office, as well as the adoption of standard methods of doing all operations which are repeated, is a matter of importance, so that under similar conditions the same appliances and methods shall be used throughout the plant. This is an absolutely necessary preliminary to success in assigning daily tasks which are fair and which can be carried out with certainty.

(k) MAINTENANCE OF SYSTEM AND PLANT, AND USE OF THE TICKLER.

One of the most important functions of the planning room is that of the maintenance of the entire system, and of standard methods and appliances throughout the establishment, including the planning room itself. An elaborate time table should be made out showing daily the time when and place where each report is due, which is necessary to carry on the work and to maintain the system. It should be the duty of the member of the planning room in charge of this function to find out at each time through the day when reports are due, whether they have been received, and if not, to keep bothering the man who is behind hand until he has done his duty. Almost all of the reports, etc., going in and out of the planning room can be made to pass through this man. As a mechanical aid to him in performing his function the tickler is invaluable. The best type of tickler is one which has a portfolio for each day in the year, large enough to insert all reminders and even quite large instruction cards and reports without folding. In maintaining methods and appliances, notices should be placed in the tickler in advance, to come out at proper intervals throughout the year for the inspection of each element of the system and the inspection and overhauling of all standards as well as the examination and repairs at stated intervals of parts of machines, boilers, engines, belts, etc., likely to wear out or give trouble, thus preventing breakdowns and delays. One tickler can be used for the entire works and is preferable to a number of individual ticklers. Each man can remind himself of his various small routine duties to be performed either daily or weekly, etc., and which might be otherwise overlooked, by sending small reminders, written on slips of paper, to be placed in the tickler and returned to him at the proper time. Both the tickler and a thoroughly systematized messenger service should be immediately adjacent to this man in the planning room, if not directly under his management.

The proper execution of this function of the planning room will relieve the superintendent of some of the most vexatious and time-consuming of his duties, and at the same time the work will be done more thoroughly and cheaper than if he does it himself. By the adoption of standards and the use of instruction cards for overhauling machinery, etc., and the use of a tickler as above described, the writer reduced the repair force of the Midvale Steel Works to one-third its size while he was in the position of master mechanic. There was no planning department, however, in the works at that time.

(l) MESSENGER SYSTEM AND POST OFFICE DELIVERY.

The messenger system should be thoroughly organized and records kept showing which of the boys are the most efficient. This should afford one of the best opportunities for selecting boys fit to be taught trades, as apprentices or otherwise. There should be a regular half hourly post office delivery system for collecting and distributing routine reports and records and messages in no especial hurry throughout the works.

(m) EMPLOYMENT BUREAU.

The selection of the men who are employed to fill vacancies or new positions should receive the most careful thought and attention and should be under the supervision of a competent man who will inquire into the experience and especial fitness and character of applicants and keep constantly revised lists of men suitable for the various positions in the shop. In this section of the planning room. an individual record of each of the men in the works can well be kept showing his punctuality, absence without excuse, violation of shop rules, spoiled work or damage to machines or tools, as well as his skill at various kinds of work; average earnings, and other good qualities for the use of this department as well as the shop disciplinarian.

(n) THE SHOP DISCIPLINARIAN.

This man may well be closely associated with the employment bureau and, if the works is not too large, the two functions can be performed by the same man. The knowledge of character and of the qualities needed for various positions acquired in disciplining the men should be useful in selecting them for employment. This man should, of course, consult constantly with the various foremen and bosses, both in his function as disciplinarian arid in the employment of men.

(o) A MUTUAL ACCIDENT INSURANCE ASSOCIATION.

A mutual accident insurance association should be established, to which the company contributes as well as the men. The object of this association is twofold: first the relief of men who are injured, and second, an opportunity of returning to the workmen all fines which are imposed upon them in disciplining them, and for damage to company's property or work spoiled.

(p) RUSH ORDER DEPARTMENT.

Hurrying through parts which have been spoiled or have developed defects, and also special repair orders for customers, should receive the attention of one man.

(q) IMPROVEMENT OF SYSTEM OR PLANT.

One man should be especially charged with the work of improvement in the system and in the running of the plant.

The type of organization described in the foregoing paragraphs has such an appearance of complication and there are so many new positions outlined in the planning room which do not exist even in a well managed establishment of the old school, that it seems desirable to again call attention to the fact that, with the exception of the study of unit times and one or two minor functions, each item of work which is performed in the planning room with the superficial appearance of great complication must also be performed by the workmen in the shop under the old type of management, with its single cheap foreman and the appearance of great simplicity. In the first case, however, the work is done by an especially trained body of men who work together like a smoothly running machine, and in the second by a much larger number of men very poorly trained and ill-fitted for this work, and each of whom while doing it is taken away from some other job for which he is well trained. The work which is now done by one sewing machine, intricate in its appearance, was formerly done by a number of women with no apparatus beyond a simple needle and thread.

There is no question that the cost of production is lowered by separating the work of planning and the brain work as much as possible from the manual labor. When this is done, however, it is evident that the brain workers must be given sufficient work to keep them fully busy all the time. They must not be allowed to stand around for a considerable part of their time waiting for their particular kind of work to come along, as is so frequently the case.

The belief is almost universal among manufacturers that for economy the number of brain workers, or non-producers, as they are called, should be as small as possible in proportion to the number of producers, i.e., those who actually work with their hands. An examination of the most successful establishments will, however, show that the reverse is true. A number of years ago the writer made a careful study of the proportion of producers to non-producers in three of the largest and most successful companies in the world, who were engaged in doing the same work in a general way. One of these companies was in France, one in Germany, and one in the United States. Being to a certain extent rivals in business and situated in different countries, naturally neither one had anything to do with the management of the other. In the course of his investigation, the writer found that the managers had never even taken the trouble to ascertain the exact proportion of non-producers to producers in their respective works; so that the organization of each company was an entirely independent evolution.

By non-producers the writer means such employees as all of the general officers, the clerks, foremen, gang bosses, watchmen, messenger boys, draftsmen, salesmen, etc.; and by "producers," only those who actually work with their hands.

In the French and German works there was found to be in each case one non-producer to between six and seven producers, and in the American works one non-producer to about seven producers. The writer found that in the case of another works, doing the same kind of business and whose management was notoriously bad, the proportion of non-producers to producers was one non-producer to about eleven producers. These companies all had large forges, foundries, rolling mills and machine shops turning out a miscellaneous product, much of which was machined. They turned out a highly wrought, elaborate and exact finished product, and did an extensive engineering and miscellaneous machine construction business.

In the case of a company doing a manufacturing business with a uniform and simple product for the maximum economy, the number of producers to each non-producer would of course be larger. No manager need feel alarmed then when he sees the number of non-producers increasing in proportion to producers, providing the non-producers are busy all of their time, and providing, of course, that in each case they are doing efficient work.

It would seem almost unnecessary to dwell upon the desirability of standardizing, not only all of the tools, appliances and implements throughout the works and office, but also the methods to be used in the multitude of small operations which are repeated day after day. There are many good managers of the old school, however, who feel that this standardization is not only unnecessary but that it is undesirable, their principal reason being that it is better to allow each workman to develop his individuality by choosing the particular implements and methods which suit him best. And there is considerable weight in this contention when the scheme of management is to allow each workman to do the work as he pleases and hold him responsible for results. Unfortunately, in ninety-nine out of a hundred such cases only the first part of this plan is carried out. The workman chooses his own methods and implements, but is not held in any strict sense accountable unless the quality of the work is so poor or the quantity turned out is so small as to almost amount to a scandal. In the type of management advocated by the writer, this complete standardization of all details and methods is not only desirable but absolutely indispensable as a preliminary to specifying the time in which each operation shall be done, and then insisting that it shall be done within the time allowed.

Neglecting to take the time and trouble to thoroughly standardize all of such methods and details is one of the chief causes for setbacks and failure in introducing this system. Much better results can be attained, even if poor standards be adopted, than can be reached if some of a given class of implements are the best of their kind while others are poor. It is uniformity that is required. Better have them uniformly second class than mainly first with some second and some third class thrown in at random. In the latter case the workmen will almost always adopt the pace which conforms to the third class instead of the first or second. In fact, however, it is not a matter involving any great expense or time to select in each case standard implements which shall be nearly the best or the best of their kinds. The writer has never failed to make enormous gains in the economy of running by the adoption of standards.

It was in the course of making a series of experiments with various air hardening tool steels with a view to adopting a standard for the Bethlehem works that Mr. J. Maunsel White, together with the writer, discovered the Taylor-White process of treating tool steel, which marks a distinct improvement in the art. The fact that this improvement was made not by manufacturers of tool steel, but in the course of the adoption of standards, shows both the necessity and fruitfulness of methodical and careful investigation in the choice of much neglected details. The economy to be gained through the adoption of uniform standards is hardly realized at all by the managers of this country. No better illustration of this fact is needed than that of the present condition of the cutting tools used throughout the machine shops of the United States. Hardly a shop can be found in which tools made from a dozen different qualities of steel are not used side by side, in many cases with little or no means of telling one make from another; and in addition, the shape of the cutting edge of the tool is in most cases left to the fancy of each individual workman. When one realizes that the cutting speed of the best treated air hardening steel is for a given depth of cut, feed and quality of metal being cut, say sixty feet per minute, while with the same shaped tool made from the best carbon tool steel and with the same conditions, the cutting speed will be only twelve feet per minute, it becomes apparent how little the necessity for rigid standards is appreciated.

Let us take another illustration. The machines of the country are still driven by belting. The motor drive, while it is coming, is still in the future. There is not one establishment in one hundred that does not leave the care and tightening of the belts to the judgment of the individual who runs the machine, although it is well known to all who have given any study to the subject that the most skilled machinist cannot properly tighten a belt without the use of belt clamps fitted with spring balances to properly register the tension. And the writer showed in a paper entitled "Notes on Belting" presented to The American Society of Mechanical Engineers in 1893, giving the results of an experiment tried on all of the belts in a machine shop and extending through nine years, in which every detail of the care and tightening and tension of each belt was recorded, that belts properly cared for according to a standard method by a trained laborer would average twice the pulling power and only a fraction of the interruptions to manufacture of those tightened according to the usual methods. The loss now going on throughout the country from failure to adopt and maintain standards for all small details is simply enormous.

It is, however, a good sign for the future that a firm such as Messrs. Dodge & Day of Philadelphia, who are making a specialty of standardizing machine shop details, find their time fully occupied.

What may be called the "exception principle" in management is coming more and more into use, although, like many of the other elements of this art, it is used in isolated cases, and in most instances without recognizing it as a principle which should extend throughout the entire field. It is not an uncommon sight, though a sad one, to see the manager of a large business fairly swamped at his desk with an ocean of letters and reports, on each of which he thinks that he should put his initial or stamp. He feels that by having this mass of detail pass over his desk he is keeping in close touch with the entire business. The exception principle is directly the reverse of this. Under it the manager should receive only condensed, summarized, and invariably comparative reports, covering, however, all of the elements entering into the management, and even these summaries should all be carefully gone over by an assistant before they reach the manager, and have all of the exceptions to the past averages or to the standards pointed out, both the especially good and especially bad exceptions, thus giving him in a few minutes a full view of progress which is being made, or the reverse, and leaving him free to consider the broader lines of policy and to study the character and fitness of the important men under him. The exception principle can be applied in many ways, and the writer will endeavor to give some further illustrations of it later.

The writer has dwelt at length upon the desirability of concentrating as much as possible clerical and brain work in the planning department. There is, however, one such important exception to this rule that it would seem desirable to call attention to it. As already stated, the planning room gives its orders and instructions to the men mainly in writing and of necessity must also receive prompt and reliable written returns and reports which shall enable its members to issue orders for the next movement of each piece, lay out the work for each man for the following day, properly post the balance of work and materials accounts, enter the records on cost accounts and also enter the time and pay of each man on the pay sheet. There is no question that all of this information can be given both better and cheaper by the workman direct than through the intermediary of a walking time keeper, providing the proper instruction and report system has been introduced in the works with carefully ruled and printed instruction and return cards, and particularly providing a complete mnemonic system of symbols has been adopted so as to save the workmen the necessity of doing much writing. The principle to which the writer wishes to call particular attention is that the only way in which workmen can be induced to write out all of this information accurately and promptly is by having each man write his own time while on day work and pay when on piece work on the same card on which he is to enter the other desired information, and then refusing to enter his pay on the pay sheet until after all of the required information has been correctly given by him. Under this system as soon as a workman completes a job and at quitting time, whether the job is completed or not, he writes on a printed time card all of the information needed by the planning room in connection with that job, signs it and forwards it at once to the planning room. On arriving in the planning room each time card passes through the order of work or route clerk, the balance clerk, the cost clerk, etc., on its way to the pay sheet, and unless the workman has written the desired information the card is sent back to him, and he is apt to correct and return it promptly so as to have his pay entered up. The principle is clear that if one wishes to have routine clerical work done promptly and correctly it should somehow be attached to the pay card of the man who is to give it. This principle, of course, applies to the information desired from inspectors, gang bosses and others as well as workmen, and to reports required from various clerks. In the case of reports, a pay coupon can be attached to the report which will be detached and sent to the pay sheet as soon as the report has been found correct.

Before starting to make any radical changes leading toward an improvement in the system of management, it is desirable, and for ultimate success in most cases necessary, that the directors and the important owners of an enterprise shall be made to understand, at least in a general way, what is involved in the change. They should be informed of the leading objects which the new system aims at, such, for instance, as rendering mutual the interests of employer and employee through "high wages and low labor cost," the gradual selection and development of a body of first class picked workmen who will work extra hard and receive extra high wages and be dealt with individually instead of in masses. They should thoroughly understand that this can only be accomplished through the adoption of precise and exact methods, and having each smallest detail, both as to methods and appliances, carefully selected so as to be the best of its kind. They should understand the general philosophy of the system and should see that, as a whole, it must be in harmony with its few leading ideas, and that principles and details which are admirable in one type of management have no place whatever in another. They should be shown that it pays to employ an especial corps to introduce a new system just as it pays to employ especial designers and workmen to build a new plant; that, while a new system is being introduced, almost twice the number of foremen are required as are needed to run it after it is in; that all of this costs money, but that, unlike a new plant, returns begin to come in almost from the start from improved methods and appliances as they are introduced, and that in most cases the new system more than pays for itself as it goes along; that time, and a great deal of time, is involved in a radical change in management, and that in the case of a large works if they are incapable of looking ahead and patiently waiting for from two to four years, they had better leave things just as they are, since a change of system involves a change in the ideas, point of view and habits of many men with strong convictions and prejudices, and that this can only be brought about slowly and chiefly through a series of object lessons, each of which takes time, and through continued reasoning; and that for this reason, after deciding to adopt a given type, the necessary steps should be taken as fast as possible, one after another, for its introduction. The directors should be convinced that an increase m the proportion of non-producers to producers means increased economy and not red tape, providing the non-producers are kept busy at their respective functions. They should be prepared to lose some of their valuable men who cannot stand the change and also for the continued indignant

89

protest of many of their old and trusted employees who can see nothing but extravagance in the new ways and ruin ahead. It is a matter of the first importance that, in addition to the directors of the company, all of those connected with the management should be given a broad and comprehensive view of the general objects to be attained and the means which will be employed. They should fully realize before starting on their work and should never lose sight of the fact that the great object of the new organization is to bring about two momentous changes in the men:

First. A complete revolution in their mental attitude toward their employers and their work.

Second. As a result of this change of feeling such an increase in their determination and physical activity, and such an improvement in the conditions under which the work is done as will result in many cases in their turning out from two to three times as much work as they have done in the past.

First, then, the men must be brought to see that the new system changes their employers from antagonists to friends who are working as hard as possible side by side with them, all pushing in the same direction and all helping to bring about such an increase in the output and to so cheapen the cost of production that the men will be paid permanently from thirty to one hundred per cent more than they have earned in the past, and that there will still be a good profit left over for the company. At first workmen cannot see why, if they do twice as much work as they have done, they should not receive twice the wages. When the matter is properly explained to them and they have time to think it over, they will see that in most cases the increase in output is quite as much due to the improved appliances and methods, to the maintenance of standards and to the great help which they receive from the men over them as to their own harder work. They will realize that the company must pay for the introduction of the improved system, which costs thousands of dollars, and also the salaries of the additional foremen and of the clerks, etc., in the planning room as well as tool room and other expenses and that, in addition, the company is entitled to an increased profit quite as much as the men are. All but a few of them will come to understand in a general way that under the new order of things they are cooperating with their employers to make as great a saving as possible and that they will receive permanently their fair share of this gain.

Then after the men acquiesce in the new order of things and are willing to do their part toward cheapening production, it will take time for them to change from their old easy-going ways to a higher rate of speed, and to learn to stay steadily at their work, think ahead and make every minute count. A certain percentage of them, with the best of intentions, will fail in this and find that they have no place in the new organization, while still others, and among them some of the best workers who are, however, either stupid or stubborn, can never be made to see that the new system is as good as the old; and these, too, must drop out. Let no one imagine, however, that this great change in the mental attitude of the men and the increase in their activity can be brought about by merely talking to them. Talking will be most useful—in fact indispensable—and no opportunity should be lost of explaining matters to them patiently, one man at a time, and giving them every chance to express their views.

Their real instruction, however, must come through a series of object lessons. They must be convinced that a great increase in speed is possible by seeing here and there a man among them increase his pace and double or treble his output. They must see this pace maintained until they are convinced that it is not a mere spurt; and, most important of all, they must see the men who "get there" in this way receive a proper increase in wages and become satisfied. It is only with these object lessons in plain sight that the new theories can be made to stick. It will be in presenting these object lessons and in smoothing away the difficulties so that tile high speed can be maintained, and in assisting to form public opinion in the shop, that the great efficiency of functional foremanship under the direction of the planning room will first become apparent.

In reaching the final high rate of speed which shall be steadily maintained, the broad fact should be realized that the men must pass through several distinct phases, rising from one plane of efficiency to another until the final level is reached. First they must be taught to work under an improved system of day work. Each man must learn how to give up his own particular way of doing things, adapt his methods to the many new standards, and grow accustomed to receiving and obeying directions covering details, large and small, which in the past have been left to his individual judgment. At first the workmen can see nothing in all of this but red tape and impertinent interference, and time must be allowed them to recover from their irritation, not only at this, but at every stage in their upward march. If they have been classed together and paid uniform wages for each class, the better men should be singled out and given higher wages so that they shall distinctly recognize the fact that each man is to be paid according to his individual worth. After becoming accustomed to direction in minor matters, they must gradually learn to obey instructions as to the pace at which they are to work, and grasp the idea, first, that the planning department knows accurately how long each operation should take; and second, that sooner or later they will have to work at the required speed if they expect to prosper. After they are used to following the speed instructions given them, then one at a time they can be raised to the level of maintaining a rapid pace throughout the day. And it is not until this final step has been taken that the full measure of the value of the new system will be felt by the men through daily receiving larger wages, and by the company through a materially larger output and lower cost of production. It is evident, of course, that all of the workmen in the shop will not rise together from one level to another. Those engaged in certain lines of work will have reached their final high speed while others have barely taken the first step. The efforts of the new management should not be spread out thin over the whole shop. They should rather be focused upon a few points, leaving the ninety and nine under the care of their former shepherds. After the efficiency of the men who are receiving special assistance and training has been raised to the desired level, the means for holding them there should be perfected, and they should never be allowed to lapse into their old ways. This will, of course, be accomplished in the most permanent way and rendered almost automatic, either through introducing task work with a bonus or the differential rate.

Before taking any steps toward changing methods the manager should realize that at no time during the introduction of the system should any broad, sweeping changes be made which seriously affect a large number of the workmen. It would be preposterous, for instance, in going from day to piece work to start a large number of men on piece work at the same time. Throughout the early stages of organization each change made should affect one workman only, and after the single man affected has become used to the new order of things, then change one man after another from the old system to the new, slowly at first, and rapidly as public opinion in the shop swings around under the influence of proper object lessons. Throughout a considerable part of the time, then, there will be two distinct systems of management in operation in the same shop; and in many cases it is desirable to have the men working under the new system managed by an entirely different set of foremen, etc., from those under the old.

The first step, after deciding upon the type of organization, should be the selection of a competent man to take charge of the introduction of the new system. The manager should think himself fortunate if he can get such a man at almost any price, since the task is a difficult and thankless one and but few men can be found who possess the necessary information coupled with the knowledge of men, the nerve, and the tact required for success in this work. The manager should keep himself free as far as possible from all active part in the introduction of the new system. While changes are going on it will require his entire energies to see that there is no falling off in the efficiency of the old system and that the quality and quantity of the output is kept up. The mistake which is usually made when a change in system is decided upon is that the manager and his principal assistants undertake to make all of the improvements themselves during their spare time, with the common result that weeks, months, and years go by without anything great being accomplished. The respective duties of the manager and the man in charge of improvement, and the limits of the authority of the latter should be clearly defined and agreed upon, always bearing in mind that responsibility should invariably be accompanied by its corresponding measure of authority.

The worst mistake that can be made is to refer to any part of the system as being "on trial." Once a given step is decided upon, all parties must be made to understand that it will go whether any one around the place likes it or not. In making changes in system the things that are given a "fair trial" fail, while the things that "must go," go all right.

To decide where to begin is a perplexing and bewildering problem which faces the reorganizer in management when he arrives in a large establishment. In making this decision, as in taking each subsequent step, the most important consideration, which should always be first in the mind of the reformer, is "what effect will this step have upon the workmen?" Through some means (it would almost appear some especial sense) the workman seems to scent the approach of a reformer even before his arrival in town. Their suspicions are thoroughly aroused, and they are on the alert for sweeping changes which are to be against their interests and which they are prepared to oppose from the start. Through generations of bitter experiences working men as a class have teamed to look upon all change as antagonistic to their best interests. They do not ask the object of the change, but oppose it simply as change. The first changes, therefore, should be such as to allay the suspicions of the men and convince them by actual contact that the reforms are after all rather harmless and are only such as will ultimately be of benefit to all concerned. Such improvements then as directly affect the workmen least should be started first. At the same time it must be remembered that the whole operation is of necessity so slow that the new system should be started at as many points as possible, and constantly pushed as hard as possible. In the metal working plant which we are using for purposes of illustration a start can be made at once along all of the following lines:

First. The introduction of standards throughout the works and office.

Second. The scientific study of unit times on several different kinds of work.

Third. A complete analysis of the pulling, feeding power and the proper speeding of the various machine tools throughout the place with a view of making a slide rule for properly running each machine.

Fourth. The work of establishing the system of time cards by means of which ultimately all of the desired information will be conveyed from the men to the planning room.

Fifth. Overhauling the stores issuing and receiving system so as to establish a complete running balance of materials.

Sixth. Ruling and printing the various blanks that will be required for shop returns and reports, time cards, instruction cards, expense sheets, cost sheets, pay sheet, and balance records; storeroom; tickler; and maintenance of standards, system, and plant, etc.; and starting such functions of the planning room as do not directly affect the men.

If the works is a large one, the man in charge of introducing the system should appoint a special assistant in charge of each of the above functions just as an engineer designing a new plant would start a number of draftsmen to work upon the various elements of construction. Several of these assistants will be brought into close contact with the men, who will in this way gradually get used to seeing changes going on and their suspicion, both of the new men and the methods, will have been allayed to such an extent before any changes which seriously affect them are made, that little or no determined opposition on their part need be anticipated. The most important and difficult task of the organizer will be that of selecting and training the various functional foremen who are to lead and instruct the workmen, and his success will be measured principally by his ability to mold and reach these men. They cannot be found, they must be made. They must be instructed in their new functions largely, in the beginning at least, by the organizer himself; and this instruction, to be effective, should be mainly in actually doing the work. Explanation and theory Will go a little way, but actual doing is needed to carry conviction. To illustrate: For nearly two and one-half years in the large shop of the Bethlehem Steel Company, one speed boss after another was instructed in the art of cutting metals fast on a large motor-driven lathe which was especially fitted to run at any desired speed within a very wide range. The work done in this machine was entirely connected, either with the study of cutting tools or the instruction of speed bosses. It was most interesting to see these men, principally either former gang bosses or the best workmen, gradually change from their attitude of determined and positive opposition to that in most cases of enthusiasm for, and earnest support of, the new methods. It was actually running the lathe themselves according to the new method and under the most positive and definite orders that produced the effect. The writer

96

himself ran the lathe and instructed the first few bosses. It required from three weeks to two months for each man. Perhaps the most important part of the gang boss's and foreman's education lies ill teaching them to promptly obey orders and instructions received not only from the superintendent or some official high in the company, but from any member of the planning room whose especial function it is to direct the rest of the works in his particular line; and it may be accepted as an unquestioned fact that no gang boss is fit to direct his men until after he has learned to promptly obey instructions received from any proper source, whether he likes his instructions and the instructor or not, and even although he may be convinced that he knows a much better way of doing the work. The first step is for each man to learn to obey the laws as they exist, and next, if the laws are wrong, to have them reformed in the proper way.

In starting to organize even a comparatively small shop, containing say from 75 to 100 men, it is best to begin by training in the full number of functional foremen, one for each function, since it must be remembered that about two out of three of those who are taught this work either leave of their own accord or prove unsatisfactory; and in addition, while both the workmen and bosses are adjusting themselves to their new duties, there are needed fully twice the number of bosses as are required to carry on the work after it is fully systematized.

Unfortunately, there is no means of selecting in advance those out of a number of candidates for a given work who are likely to prove successful. Many of those who appear to have all of the desired qualities, and who talk and appear the best, will turn out utter failures, while on the other hand, some of the most unlikely men rise to the top. The fact is that the more attractive qualities of good manners, education, and even special training and skill, which are more apparent on the surface, count for less in an executive position than the grit, determination and bulldog endurance and tenacity that knows no defeat and comes up smiling to be knocked down over and over again. The two qualities which count most for success in this kind of executive work are grit and what may be called "constructive imagination"—the faculty which enables a man to use the few facts that are stored in his mind in getting around the obstacles that oppose him, and in building up something useful in spite of them; and unfortunately, the presence of these qualities, together with honesty and common sense, can only be proved through an actual trial at executive work. As we all know, success at college or in the technical school does not indicate the presence of these qualities, even though the man may have worked hard. Mainly, it would seem, because the work of obtaining an education is principally that of absorption and assimilation; while that of active practical life is principally the direct reverse, namely, that of giving out.

In selecting men to be tried as foremen, or in fact for any position throughout the place, from the day laborer up, one of two different types of men should be chosen, according to the nature of the work to be done. For one class of work, men should be selected who are too good for the job; and for the other class of work, men who are barely good enough.

If the work is of a routine nature, in which the same operations are likely to be done over and over again, with no great variety, and in which there is no apparent prospect of a radical change being made, perhaps through a term of years, even though the work itself may be complicated in its nature, a man should be selected whose abilities are barely equal to the task. Time and training will fit him for his work, and since he will be better paid than in the past, and will realize that he has been given the chance to make his abilities yield him the largest return—all of the elements for promoting contentment will be present; and those men who are blessed with cheerful dispositions will become satisfied and remain so. Of course, a considerable part of mankind is so born or educated that permanent contentment is out of the question. No one, however, should be influenced by the discontent of this class.

On the other hand, if the work to be done is of great variety — particularly if improvements in methods are to be anticipated — throughout the period of active organization the men engaged in systematizing should be too good for their jobs. For such work, men should be selected whose mental caliber and attainments will fit them, ultimately at least, to command higher wages than can be afforded on the work which they are at. It will prove a wise policy to promote such men both to better positions and pay, when they have shown themselves capable of accomplishing results and the opportunity offers. The results which these high-class men will accomplish, and the comparatively short time which they will take in organizing, will much more than pay for the expense and trouble, later on, of training other men, cheaper and of less capacity, to take their places. In many cases, however, gang bosses and men will develop faster than new positions open for them. When this occurs, it will pay employers well to find them positions in other works, either with better pay, or larger opportunities; not only as a matter of kindly feeling and generosity toward their men, but even more with the object of promoting the best interests of their own establishments. For one man lost in this way, five will be stimulated to work to the very limit of their abilities, and will rise ultimately to take the place of the man who has gone, and the best class of men will apply for work where these methods prevail. But few employers, however, are sufficiently broad-minded to adopt this policy. They dread the trouble and temporary inconvenience incident to training in new men.

Mr. James M. Dodge, Chairman of the Board of the Link-Belt Company, is one of the few men with whom the writer is acquainted who has been led by his kindly instincts, as well as by a far-sighted policy, to treat his employees in this way; and this, together with the personal magnetism and influence which

99

belong to men of his type, has done much to render his shop one of the model establishments of the country, certainly as far as the relations of employer and men are concerned. On the other hand, this policy of promoting men and finding them new positions has its limits. No worse mistake can be made than that of allowing an establishment to be looked upon as a training school, to be used mainly for the education of many of its employees. All employees should bear in mind that each shop exists, first, last, and all the time, for the purpose of paying dividends to its owners. They should have patience, and never lose sight of this fact. And no man should expect promotion until after he has trained his successor to take his place. The writer is quite sure that in his own case, as a young man, no one element was of such assistance to him in obtaining new opportunities as the practice of invariably training another man to fill his position before asking for advancement.

The first of the functional foremen to be brought into actual contact with the men should be the inspector; and the whole system of inspection, with its proper safeguards, should be in smooth and successful operation before any steps are taken toward stimulating the men to a larger output; otherwise an increase in quantity will probably be accompanied by a falling off in quality.

Next choose for the application of the two principal functional foremen, viz., the speed boss and the gang boss, that portion of the work in which there is the largest need of, and opportunity for, making a gain. It is of the utmost importance that the first combined application of time study, slide rules, instruction cards, functional foremanship, and a premium for a large daily task should prove a success both for the workmen and for the company, and for this reason a simple class of work should be chosen for a start. The entire efforts of the new management should be centered on one point, and continue there until unqualified success has been attained.

When once this gain has been made, a peg should be put in which shall keep it from sliding back in the least; and it is here that the task idea with a time limit for each job will be found most useful. Under ordinary piece work, or the Towne-Halsey plan, the men are likely at any time to slide back a considerable distance without having it particularly noticed either by them or the management. With the task idea, the first falling off is instantly felt by the workman through the loss of his day's bonus, or his differential rate, and is thereby also forcibly brought to the attention of the management.

There is one rather natural difficulty which arises when the functional foremanship is first introduced. Men who were formerly either gang bosses, or foremen, are usually chosen as functional foremen, and these men, when they find their duties restricted to their particular functions, while they formerly were called upon to do everything, at first feel dissatisfied. They think that their field of usefulness is being greatly contracted. This is, however, a theoretical difficulty, which disappears when they really get into the full swing of their new positions. In fact the new position demands an amount of special information, forethought, and a clear-cut, definite responsibility that they have never even approximated in the past, and which is amply sufficient to keep all of their best faculties and energies alive and fully occupied. It is the experience of the writer that there is a great commercial demand for men with this sort of definite knowledge, who are used to accepting real responsibility and getting results; so that the training in their new duties renders them more instead of less valuable.

As a rule, the writer has found that those who were growling the most, and were loudest in asserting that they ought to be doing the whole thing, were only one-half or one-quarter performing their own particular functions. This desire to do every one's else work in addition to their own generally disappears when they are held to strict account in their particular line, and are given enough work to keep them hustling.

There are many people who will disapprove of the whole scheme of a planning department to do the thinking for the men, as well as a number of foremen to assist and lead each man in his work, on the ground that this does not tend to promote independence, self-reliance, and originality in the individual. Those holding this view, however, must take exception to the whole trend of modern industrial development; and it appears to the writer that they overlook the real facts in the case.

It is true, for instance, that the planning room, and functional foremanship, render it possible for an intelligent laborer or helper in time to do much of the work now done by a machinist. Is not this a good thing for the laborer and helper? He is given a higher class of work, which tends to develop him and gives him better wages. In the sympathy for the machinist the case of the laborer is overlooked. This sympathy for the machinist is, however, wasted, since the machinist, with the aid of the new system, will rise to a higher class of work which he was unable to do in the past, and in addition, divided or functional foremanship will call for a larger number of men in this class, so that men, who must otherwise have remained machinists all their lives, will have the opportunity of rising to a foremanship.

The demand for men of originality and brains was never so great as it is now, and the modern subdivision of labor, instead of dwarfing men, enables them all along the line to rise to a higher plane of efficiency, involving at the same time more brain work and less monotony. The type of man who was formerly a day laborer and digging dirt is now for instance making shoes in a shoe factory. The dirt handling is done by Italians or Hungarians.

After the planning room with functional foremanship has accomplished its most difficult task, of teaching the men how to do a full day's work themselves, and also how to get it out of their machines steadily, then, if desired, the number of non-producers can be diminished, preferably, by giving each type of functional foreman more to do in his specialty; or in the case of a very small shop, by combining two different functions in the same man. The former expedient is, however, much to be preferred to the latter. There need never be any worry about what is to become of those engaged in systematizing after the period of active organization is over. The difficulty will still remain even with functional foremanship, that of getting enough good men to fill the positions, and the demand for competent gang bosses will always be so great that no good boss need look for a job.

Of all the farces in management the greatest is that of an establishment organized along well planned lines, with all of the elements needed for success, and yet which fails to get either output or economy. There must be some man or men present in the organization who will not mistake the form for the essence, and who will have brains enough to find out those of their employees who "get there," and nerve enough to make it unpleasant for those who fail, as well as to reward those who succeed. No system can do away with the need of real men. Both system and good men are needed, and after introducing the best system, success will be in proportion to the ability, consistency, and respected authority of the management.

In a book of this sort, it would be manifestly impossible to discuss at any length all of the details which go toward making the system a success. Some of them are of such importance as to render at least a brief reference to them necessary. And first among these comes the study of unit times.

This, as already explained, is the most important element of the system advocated by the writer. Without it, the definite, clear-cut directions given to the workman, and the assigning of a full, yet just, daily task, with its premium for success, would be impossible; and the arch without the keystone would fall to the ground.

In 1883, while foreman of the machine shop of the Midvale Steel Company of Philadelphia, it occurred to the writer that it was simpler to time with a stop watch each of the elements of the various kinds of work done in the place, and then find the quickest time in which each job could be done by summing up the total times of its component parts, than it was to search through the time records of former jobs and guess at the proper time and price. After practicing this method of time study himself for about a year, as well as circumstances would permit, it became evident that the system was a success.

The writer then established the time-study and rate-fixing department, which has given out piece work prices in the place ever since.

This department far more than paid for itself from the very start; but it was several years before the full benefits of the system were felt, owing to the fact that the best methods of making and recording time observations, as well as of determining the maximum capacity of each of the machines in the place, and of making working tables and time tables, were not at first adopted.

It has been the writer's experience that the difficulties of scientific time study are underestimated at first, and greatly overestimated after actually trying the work for two or three months. The average manager who decides to undertake the study of unit times in his works fails at first to realize that he is starting a new art or trade. He understands, for instance, the difficulties which he would meet with in establishing a drafting room, and would look for but small results at first, if he were to give a bright man the task of making drawings, who had never worked in a drafting room, and who was not even familiar with drafting implements and methods, but he entirely underestimates the difficulties of this new trade.

The art of studying unit times is quite as important and as

difficult as that of the draftsman. It should be undertaken seriously, and looked upon as a profession. It has its own peculiar implements and methods, without the use and understanding of which progress will necessarily be slow, and in the absence of which there will be more failures than successes scored at first.

When, on the other hand, an energetic, determined man goes at time study as if it were his life's work, with the determination to succeed, the results which he can secure are little short of astounding. The difficulties of the task will be felt at once and so strongly by any one who undertakes it, that it seems important to encourage the beginner by giving at least one illustration of what has been accomplished.

Mr. Sanford E. Thompson, C. E., started in 1896 with but small help from the writer, except as far as the implements and methods are concerned, to study the time required to do all kinds of work in the building trades. In six years he has made a complete study of eight of the most important trades— excavation, masonry (including sewer-work and paving), carpentry, concrete and cement work, lathing and plastering, slating and roofing and rock quarrying. He took every stop watch observation himself and then, with the aid of two comparatively cheap assistants, worked up and tabulated all of his data ready for the printer. The magnitude of this undertaking will be appreciated when it is understood that the tables and descriptive matter for one of these trades alone take up about 250 pages. Mr. Thompson and the writer are both engineers, but neither of us was especially familiar with the above trades, and this work could not have been accomplished in a lifetime without the study of elementary units with a stop watch.

In the course of this work, Mr. Thompson has developed what are in many respects the best implements in use, and with his permission some of them will be described. The blank form or note sheet used by Mr. Thompson, shown in Fig. 2 (see page

151), contains essentially: [Transcriber's note — Figure 2 omitted]

(1) Space for the description of the work and notes in regard to it.

(2) A place for recording the total time of complete operations— that is, the gross time including all necessary delays, for doing a whole job or large portions of it.

(3) Lines for setting down the "detail operations, or units" into which any piece of work may be divided, followed by columns for entering the averages obtained from the observations.

(4) Squares for recording the readings of the stop watch when observing the times of these elements. If these squares are filled, additional records can be entered on the back. The size of the sheets, which should be of best quality ledger paper, is 8 3/4 inches wide by 7 inches long, and by folding in the center they can be conveniently carried in the pocket, or placed in a case (see Fig. 3, page 153) containing one or more stop watches.

This case, or "watch book," is another device of Mr. Thompson's. It consists of a frame work, containing concealed in it one, two, or three watches, whose stop and start movements can be operated by pressing with the fingers of the left hand upon the proper portion of the cover of the note-book without the knowledge of the workman who is being observed. The frame is bound in a leather case resembling a pocket note-book, and has a place for the note sheets described.

The writer does not believe at all in the policy of spying upon the workman when taking time observations for the purpose of time study. If the men observed are to be ultimately affected by the results of these observations, it is generally best to come out openly, and let them know that they are being timed, and what the object of the timing is. There are many cases, however, in which telling the workman that he was being timed in a minute

106

way would only result in a row, and in defeating the whole object of the timing; particularly when only a few time units are to be studied on one man's work, and when this man will not be personally affected by the results of the observations. In these cases, the watch book of Mr. Thompson, holding the watches in the cover, is especially useful. A good deal of judgment is required to know when to time openly, or the reverse.

FIGURE 3. -WATCH BOOK FOR TIME STUDY

[Transcriber's note — Figure 3 omitted]

The operation selected for illustration on the note sheet shown in Fig. 2, page 151, is the excavation of earth with wheelbarrows, and the values given are fair averages of actual contract work where the wheelbarrow man fills his own barrow. It is obvious that similar methods of analyzing and recording may be applied to work ranging from unloading coal to skilled labor on fine machine tools.

The method of using the note sheets for timing a workman is as follows:

After entering the necessary descriptive matter at the top of the sheet, divide the operation to be timed into its elementary units, and write these units one after another under the heading "Detail Operations." If the job is long and complicated, it may be analyzed while the timing is going on, and the elementary units entered then instead of beforehand. In wheelbarrow work as illustrated in the example shown on the note sheet, the elementary units consist of "filling barrow," "starting" (which includes throwing down shovel and lifting handles of barrow), "wheeling full," etc. These units might have been further subdivided—the first one into time for loading one shovelful, or still further into the time for filling and the time for emptying each shovelful. The letters a, b, c, etc., which are printed, are simply for convenience in designating the elements.

107

We are now ready for the stop watch, which, to save clerical work, should be provided with a decimal dial similar to that shown in Fig. 4. The method of using this and recording the times depends upon the character of the time observations. In all cases, however, the stop watch times are recorded in the columns headed "Time" at the top of the right-hand half of the note sheet. These columns are the only place on the face of the sheet where stop watch readings are to be entered. If more space is required for these times, they should be entered on the back of the sheet. The rest of the figures (except those on the left-hand side of the note sheet, which may be taken from an ordinary timepiece) are the results of calculation, and may be made in the office by any clerk.

FIGURE 4. -STOP WATCH WITH DECIMAL FACE

[Transcriber's note — omitted]

As has been stated, the method of recording the stop watch observations depends upon the work which is being observed. If the operation consists of the same element repeated over and over, the time of each may be set down separately; or, if the element is very small, the total time of, say, ten may be entered as a fraction, with the time for all ten observations as the numerator, and the number of observations for the denominator.

In the illustration given on the note sheet, Fig. 2, the operation consists of a series of elements. In such a case, the letters designating each elementary unit are entered under the columns "Op.," the stop watch is thrown to zero, and started as the man commences to work. As each new division of the operation (that is, as each elementary unit or unit time) is begun, the time is recorded. During any special delay the watch may be stopped, and started again from the same point, although, as a rule, Mr. Thompson advocates allowing the watch to run continuously, and enters the time of such a stop, designating it for convenience by the letter "Y."

In the case we are considering, two kinds of materials were handled sand and clay. The time of each of the unit times, except the "filling," is the same for both sand and clay; hence, if we have sufficient observations on either one of the materials, the only element of the other which requires to be timed is the loading. This illustrates one of the merits of the elementary system.

The column "Av." is filled from the preceding column. The figures thus found are the actual net times of the different unit times. These unit times are averaged and entered in the "Time" column, on the lower half of the right-hand page, preceded, in the "No." column, by the number of observations which have been taken of each unit. These times, combined and compared with the gross times on the left-hand page, will determine the percentage lost in resting and other necessary delays. A convenient method for obtaining the time of an operation, like picking, in which the quantity is difficult to measure, is suggested by the records on the left-hand page.

The percentage of the time taken in rest and other necessary delays, which is noted on the sheet as, in this case, about 27 per cent, is obtained by a comparison of the average net "time per barrow" on the right with the "time per barrow" on the left. The latter is the quotient of the total time shoveling and wheeling divided by the number of loads wheeled.

It must be remembered that the example given is simply for illustration. To obtain accurate average times, for any item of work under specified conditions, it is necessary to take observations upon a number of men, each of whom is at work under conditions which are comparable. The total number of observations which should be taken of any one elementary unit depends upon its variableness, and also upon its frequency of occurrence in a day's work.

An expert observer can, on many kinds of work, time two or three men at the same time with the same watch, or he can operate two or three watches—one for each man. A note sheet can contain only a comparatively few observations. It is not convenient to make it of larger size than the dimensions given, when a watch-book is to be used, although it is perfectly feasible to make the horizontal rulings 8 lines to the inch instead of 5 lines to the inch as on the sample sheet. There will have to be, in almost all cases, a large number of note sheets on the same subject. Some system must be arranged for collecting and tabulating these records. On Tables 2A and 2B (pages 160 and 161) is shown the form used for tabulating. The length should be either 17 or 22 inches. The height of the form is 11 inches. With these dimensions a form may be folded and filed with ordinary letter sheets (8 1/2 inches by 11 inches). The ruling which has been found most convenient is for the vertical divisions 3 columns to 1 1/8 inches, while the horizontal lines are ruled 6 to the inch. The columns may, or may not, have printed headings.

The data from the note sheet in Fig. 2 (page 151) is copied on to the table for illustration. The first columns of the table are descriptive. The rest of them are arranged so as to include all of the unit times, with any other data which are to be averaged or used when studying the results. At the extreme right of the sheet the gross times, including rest and necessary delay, are recorded and the percentages of rest are calculated.

Formulae are convenient for combining the elements. For simplicity, in the example of barrow excavation, each of the unit times may be designated by the same letters used on the note sheet (Fig. 2) although in practice each element can best be designated .by the initial letters of the words describing it.

Let

a = time filling a barrow with any material.

b = time preparing to wheel.

c = time wheeling full barrow 100 feet.

110

d = time dumping and turning.

e = time returning 100 feet with empty barrow.

f = time dropping barrow and starting to shovel.

p = time loosening one cubic yard with the pick.

P = percentage of a day required to rest and necessary delays.

L = load of a barrow in cubic feet.

B = time per cubic yard picking, loading, and wheeling any given kind of earth to any given distance when the wheeler loads his own barrow.

[Transcriber's note — formula and Tables omitted]

This general formula for barrow work can be simplified by choosing average values for the constants, and substituting numerals for the letters now representing them. Substituting the average values from the note sheet on Fig. 2 (page 151), our formula becomes: [Transcriber's note — formula omitted]

In classes of work where the percentage of rest varies with the different elements of an operation it is most convenient to correct all of the elementary times by the proper percentages before combining them. Sometimes after having constructed a general formula, it may be solved by setting down the substitute numerical values in a vertical column for direct addition.

Table 3 (page 164) gives the times for throwing earth to different distances and different heights. It will be seen that for each special material the time for filling shovel remains the same regardless of the distance to which it is thrown. Each kind of material requires a different time for filling the shovel. The time throwing one shovelful, on the other hand, varies with the length of throw, but for any given distance it is the same for all of the earths. If the earth is of such a nature that it sticks to the

111

shovel, this relation does not hold. For the elements of shoveling we have therefore:

s = time filling shovel and straightening up ready to throw.

t = time throwing one shovelful.

w = time walking one foot with loaded shovel.

w1 = time returning one foot with empty shovel.

L = load of a shovel in cubic feet.

P = percentage of a day required for rest and necessary delays.

T = time for shoveling one cubic yard.

Our formula, then, for handling any earth after it is loosened, is:

[Transcriber's note — omitted]

Where the material is simply thrown without walking, the formula becomes:

If weights are used instead of volumes:

[Transcriber's note — omitted]

The writer has found the printed form shown on the insert, Fig. 5 (opposite page 166), useful in studying unit times in a certain class of the hand work done in a machine shop. This blank is fastened to a thin board held in the left hand and resting on the left arm of the observer. A stop watch is inserted in a small compartment attached to the back of the board at a point a little above its center, the face of the watch being seen from the front of the board through a small flap cut partly loose from the observation blank. While the watch is operated by the fingers of the left hand, the right hand of the operator is at all times free to enter the time observations on the blank. A pencil sketch of the work to be observed is made in the blank space on the upper left-hand portion of the sheet. In using this blank, of course, all attempt at secrecy is abandoned.

The mistake usually made by beginners is that of failing to note in sufficient detail the various conditions surrounding the job. It is not at first appreciated that the whole work of the time observer is useless if there is any doubt as to even one of these conditions. Such items, for instance, as the name of the man or men on the work, the number of helpers, and exact description of all of the implements used, even those which seem unimportant, such, for instance, as the diameter and length of bolts and the style of clamps used, the weight of the piece upon which work is being done, etc.

It is also desirable that, as soon as practicable after taking a few complete sets of time observations, the operator should be given the opportunity of working up one or two sets at least by summing up the unit times and allowing the proper per cent of rest, etc., and putting them into practical use, either by comparing his results with the actual time of a job which is known to be done in fast time, or by setting a time which a workman is to live up to.

The actual practical trial of the time student's work is most useful, both in teaching him the necessity of carefully noting the minutest details, and on the other hand convincing him of the practicability of the whole method, and in encouraging him in future work.

In making time observations, absolutely nothing should be left to the memory of the student. Every item, even those which appear self-evident, should be accurately recorded. The writer, and the assistant who immediately followed him, both made the mistake of not putting the results of much of their time study into use soon enough, so that many times observations which extended over a period of months were thrown away, in most instances because of failure to note some apparently unimportant detail.

It may be needless to state that when the results of time observations are first worked up, it will take far more time to pick out and add up the proper unit times, and allow the proper percentages of rest, etc., than it originally did for the workman to do the job. This fact need not disturb the operator, however. It will be evident that the slow time made at the start is due to his lack of experience, and he must take it for granted that later many short-cuts can be found, and that a man with an average memory will be able with practice to carry all of the important time units in his head.

No system of time study can be looked upon as a success unless it enables the time observer, after a reasonable amount of study, to predict with accuracy how long it should take a good man to do almost any job in the particular trade, or branch of a trade, to which the time student has been devoting himself. It is true that hardly any two jobs in a given trade are exactly the same and that if a time student were to follow the old method of studying and recording the whole time required to do the various jobs which came under his observation, without dividing them into their elements, he would make comparatively small progress in a lifetime, and at best would become a skilful guesser. It is, however, equally true that all of the work done in a given trade can be divided into a comparatively small number of elements or units, and that with proper implements arid methods it is comparatively easy for a skilled observer to determine the time required by a good man to do any one of these elementary units.

Having carefully recorded the time for each of these elements, it is a simple matter to divide each job into its elementary units, and by adding their times together, to arrive accurately at the total time for the job. The elements of the art which at first appear most difficult to investigate are the percentages which should be allowed, under different conditions, for rest and for accidental or unavoidable delays. These elements can, however, be studied with about the same accuracy as the others.

Perhaps the greatest difficulty rests upon the fact that no two men work at exactly the same speed. The writer has found it best to take his time observations on first-class men only, when they can be found; and these men should be timed when working at their best. Having obtained the best time of a first-class man, it is a simple matter to determine the percentage which an average man will fall short of this maximum.

It is a good plan to pay a first-class man an extra price while his work is being timed. When work men once understand that the time study is being made to enable them to earn higher wages, the writer has found them quite ready to help instead of hindering him in his work. The division of a given job into its proper elementary units, before beginning the time study, calls for considerable skill and good judgment. If the job to be observed is one which will be repeated over and over again, or if it is one of a series of similar jobs which form an important part of the standard work of an establishment, or of the trade which is being studied, then it is best to divide the job into elements which are rudimentary. In some cases this subdivision should be carried to a point which seems at first glance almost absurd.

For example, in the case of the study of the art of shoveling earths, referred to in Table 3, page 164, it will be seen that handling a shovelful of dirt is subdivided into, s = "Time filling shovel and straightening up ready to throw," and t = "Time throwing one shovelful."

The first impression is that this minute subdivision of the work into elements, neither of which takes more than five or six seconds to perform, is little short of preposterous; yet if a rapid and thorough time study of the art of shoveling is to be made, this subdivision simplifies the work, and makes time study quicker and more thorough.

The reasons for this are twofold:

First. In the art of shoveling dirt, for instance, the study of fifty or sixty small elements, like those referred to above, will enable one to fix the exact time for many thousands of complete jobs of shoveling, constituting a very considerable proportion of the entire art.

Second. The study of single small elements is simpler, quicker, and more certain to be successful than that of a large number of elements combined. The greater the length of time involved in a single item of time study, the greater will be the likelihood of interruptions or accidents, which will render the results obtained by the observer questionable or even useless.

There is a considerable part of the work of most establishments that is not what may be called standard work, namely, that which is repeated many times. Such jobs as this can be divided for time study into groups, each of which contains several rudimentary elements. A division of this sort will be seen by referring to the data entered on face of note sheet, Fig. 2 (page 151).

In this case, instead of observing, first, the "time to fill a shovel," and then the time to "throw it into a wheelbarrow," etc., a number of these more rudimentary operations are grouped into the single operation of

a = "Time filling a wheelbarrow with any material."

This group of operations is thus studied as a whole.

Another illustration of the degree of subdivision which is desirable will be found by referring to the inserts, Fig. 5 (opposite page 166).

Where a general study is being made of the time required to do all kinds of hand work connected with and using machine tools, the items printed in detail should be timed singly.

116

When some special job, not to be repeated many times, is to be studied, then several elementary items can be grouped together and studied as a whole, in such groups for example as:

(a) Getting job ready to set.

(b) Setting work.

(c) Setting tool.

(d) Extra hand work.

(e) Removing work.

And in some cases even these groups can be further condensed.

An illustration of the time units which it is desirable to sum up and properly record and index for a certain kind of lathe work is given in Fig. 6.

SIGNED TOTAL FIGURE 6. -INSTRUCTION CARD FOR LATHE WORK (not shown)

The writer has found that when some jobs are divided into their proper elements, certain of these elementary operations are so very small in time that it is difficult, if not impossible, to obtain accurate readings on the watch. In such cases, where the work consists of recurring cycles of elementary operations, that is, where a series of elementary operations is repeated over and over again, it is possible to take sets of observations on two or more of the successive elementary operations which occur in regular order, and from the times thus obtained to calculate the time of each element. An example of this is the work of loading pig iron on to bogies. The elementary operations or elements consist of:

(a) Picking up a pig.

(b) Walking with it to the bogie.

117

(c) Throwing or placing it on the bogie.

(d) Returning to the pile of pigs.

Here the length of time occupied in picking up the pig and throwing or placing it on the bogie is so small as to be difficult to time, but observations may be taken successively on the elements in sets of three. We may, in other words, take one set of observations upon the combined time of the three elements numbered 1, 2, 3; another set upon elements 2, 3, 4; another set upon elements, 3, 4, 1, and still another upon the set 4,1, 2. By algebraic equations we may solve the values of each of the separate elements.

If we take a cycle consisting of five (5) elementary operations, a, b, c, d, e, and let observations be taken on three of them at a time, we have the equations:

[Transcriber's Note: omitted]

The writer was surprised to find, however, that while in some cases these equations were readily solved, in others they were impossible of solution. My friend, Mr. Carl G. Barth, when the matter was referred to him, soon developed the fact that the number of elements of a cycle which may be observed together is subject to a mathematical law, which is expressed by him as follows:

The number of successive elements observed together must be prime to the total number of elements in the cycle.

Namely, the number of elements in any set must contain no factors; that is, must be divisible by no numbers which are contained in the total number of elements. The following table is, therefore, calculated by Mr. Barth showing how many operations may be observed together in various cases. The last column gives the number of observations in a set which will lead to the determination of the results with the minimum of labor.

118

[Transcriber's note — Table omitted]

When time study is undertaken in a systematic way, it becomes possible to do greater justice in many ways both to employers and workmen than has been done in the past. For example, we all know that the first time that even a skilled workman does a job it takes him a longer time than is required after he is familiar with his work, and used to a particular sequence of operations. The practiced time student can not only figure out the time in which a piece of work should be done by a good man, after he has become familiar with this particular job through practice, but he should also be able to state how much more time would be required to do the same job when a good man goes at it for the first time; and this knowledge would make it possible to assign one time limit and price for new work, and a smaller time and price for the same job after being repeated, which is much more fair and just to both parties than the usual fixed price.

As the writer has said several times, the difference between the best speed of a first-class man and the actual speed of the average man is very great. One of the most difficult pieces of work which must be faced by the man who is to set the daily tasks is to decide just how hard it is wise for him to make the task. Shall it be fixed for a first-class man, and if not, then at what point between the first-class and the average? One fact is clear, it should always be well above the performance of the average man, since men will invariably do better if a bonus is offered them than they have done without this incentive. The writer has, in almost all cases, solved this part of the problem by fixing a task which required a first-class man to do his best, and then offering a good round premium. When this high standard is set it takes longer to raise the men up to it. But it is surprising after all how rapidly they develop.

The precise point between the average and the first-class, which is selected for the task, should depend largely upon the labor market in which the works is situated. If the works were in a fine labor market, such, for instance, as that of Philadelphia, there is no question that the highest standard should be aimed at. If, on the other hand, the shop required a good deal of skilled labor, and was situated in a small country town, it might be wise to aim rather lower. There is a great difference in the labor markets of even some of the adjoining states in this country, and in one instance, in which the writer was aiming at a high standard in organizing a works, he found it necessary to import almost all of his men from a neighboring state before meeting with success.

Whether the bonus is given only when the work is done in the quickest time or at some point between this and the average time, in all cases the instruction card should state the best time in which the work can be done by a first-class man. There will then be no suspicion on the part of the men when a longer "bonus time" is allowed that the time student does not really know the possibilities of the case. For example, the instruction card might read:

Proper time . . . . . 65 minutes

Bonus given first time job is done. 108 minutes

It is of the greatest importance that the man who has charge of assigning tasks should be perfectly straightforward in all of his dealings with the men. Neither in this nor in any other branch of the management should a man make any pretense of having more knowledge than he really possesses. He should impress the workmen with the fact that he is dead in earnest, and that he fully intends to know all about it some day; but he should make no claim to omniscience, and should always be ready to acknowledge and correct an error if he makes one. This combination of determination and frankness establishes a sound and healthy relation between the management and men.

There is no class of work which cannot be profitably submitted to time study, by dividing it into its time elements, except such operations as take place in the head of the worker; and the writer has even seen a time study made of the speed of an average and first-class boy in solving problems in mathematics.

Clerk work can well be submitted to time study, and a daily task assigned in work of this class which at first appears to be very miscellaneous in its character.

One of the needs of modern management is that of literature on the subject of time study. The writer quotes as follows from his paper on "A Piece Rate System," written in 1895:

"Practically the greatest need felt in an establishment wishing to start a rate-fixing department is the lack of data as to the proper rate of speed at which work should be done. There are hundreds of operations which are common to most large establishments, yet each concern studies the speed problem for itself, and days of labor are wasted in what should be settled once for all, and recorded in a form which is available to all manufacturers.

"What is needed is a hand-book on the speed with which work can be done, similar to the elementary engineering handbooks. And the writer ventures to predict that such a book will before long be forthcoming. Such a book should describe the best method of making, recording, tabulating, and indexing time observations, since much time and effort are wasted by the adoption of inferior methods."

Unfortunately this prediction has not yet been realized. The writer's chief object in inducing Mr. Thompson to undertake a scientific time study of the various building trades and to join him in a publication of this work was to demonstrate on a large scale not only the desirability of accurate time study, but the efficiency and superiority of the method of studying elementary units as outlined above. He trusts that his object may be realized and that the publication of this book may be followed by similar works on other trades and more particularly on the details of machine shop practice, in which he is especially interested.

As a machine shop has been chosen to illustrate the application of such details of scientific management as time study, the planning department, functional foremanship, instruction cards, etc., the description would be far from complete without at least a brief reference to the methods employed in solving the time problem for machine tools.

The study of this subject involved the solution of four important problems:

First. The power required to cut different kinds of metals with tools of various shapes when using different depths of cut and coarseness of feed, and also the power required to feed the tool under varying conditions.

Second. An investigation of the laws governing the cutting of metals with tools, chiefly with the object of determining the effect upon the best cutting speed of each of the following variables:

(a) The quality of tool steel and treatment of tools (i.e., in heating, forging, and tempering them).

(b) The shape of tool (i.e., the curve or line of the cutting edge, the lip angle, and clearance angle)

(c) The duration of cut or the length of time the tool is required to last before being re-ground.

(d) The quality or hardness of the metal being cut (as to its effect on cutting speed).

(e) The depth of the cut.

(f) The thickness of the feed or shaving

(g) The effect on cutting speed of using water or other cooling medium on the tool.

122

Third. The best methods of analyzing the driving and feeding power of machine tools and, after considering their limitations as to speeds and feeds, of deciding upon the proper counter-shaft or other general driving speeds.

Fourth. After the study of the first, second, and third problems had resulted in the discovery of certain clearly defined laws, which were expressed by mathematical formulae, the last and most difficult task of all lay in finding a means for solving the entire problem which should be so practical and simple as to enable an ordinary mechanic to answer quickly and accurately for each machine in the shop the question, "What driving speed, feed, and depth of cut will in each particular case do the work in the quickest time?"

In 1881, in the machine shop of the Midvale Steel Company, the writer began a systematic study of the laws involved in the first and second problems above referred to by devoting the entire time of a large vertical boring mill to this work, with special arrangements for varying the drive so as to obtain any desired speed. The needed uniformity of the metal was obtained by using large locomotive tires of known chemical composition, physical properties and hardness, weighing from 1,500 to 2,000 pounds.

For the greater part of the succeeding 22 years these experiments were carried on, first at Midvale and later in several other shops, under the general direction of the writer, by his friends and assistants, six machines having been at various times especially fitted up for this purpose.

The exact determination of these laws and their reduction to formulae have proved a slow but most interesting problem; but by far the most difficult undertaking has been the development of the methods and finally the appliances (i.e., slide rules) for making practical use of these laws after they were discovered.

In 1884 the writer succeeded in making a slow solution of this problem with the help of his friend, Mr. Geo. M. Sinclair, by indicating the values of these variables through curves and laying down one set of curves over another. Later my friend, Mr. H. L. Gantt, after devoting about 1 1/2 years exclusively to this work, obtained a much more rapid and simple solution. It was not, however, until 1900, in the works of the Bethlehem Steel Company, that Mr. Carl G. Barth, with the assistance of Mr. Gantt and a small amount of help from the writer, succeeded in developing a slide rule by means of which the entire problem can be accurately and quickly solved by any mechanic.

The difficulty from a mathematical standpoint of obtaining a rapid and accurate solution of this problem will be appreciated when it is remembered that twelve independent variables enter into each problem, and that a change in any of these will affect the answer. The instruction card can be put to wide and varied use. It is to the art of management what the drawing is to engineering, and, like the latter, should vary in size and form according to the amount and variety of the information which it is to convey. In some cases it should consist of a pencil memorandum on a small piece of paper which will be sent directly to the man requiring the instructions, while in others it will be in the form of several pages of typewritten matter, properly varnished and mounted, and issued under the check or other record system, so that it can be used time after time. A description of an instruction card of this kind may be useful.

After the writer had become convinced of the economy of standard methods and appliances, and the desirability of relieving the men as far as possible from the necessity of doing the planning, while master mechanic at Midvale, he tried to get his assistant to write a complete instruction card for overhauling and cleaning the boilers at regular periods, to be sure that the inspection was complete, and that while the work was thoroughly done, the boilers should be out of use as short a time as possible, and also to have the various elements of this work done on piece work instead of by the day. His assistant, not having undertaken work of this kind before, failed at it, and the writer was forced to do it himself. He did all of the work of chipping, cleaning, and overhauling a set of boilers and at the same time made a careful time study of each of the elements of the work. This time study showed that a great part of the time was lost owing to the constrained position of the workman. Thick pads were made to fasten to the elbows, knees, and hips; special tools and appliances were made for the various details of the work; a complete list of the tools and implements was entered on the instruction card, each tool being stamped with its own number for identification, and all were issued from the tool room in a tool box so as to keep them together and save time. A separate piece work price was fixed for each of the elements of the job and a thorough inspection of each part of the work secured as it was completed.

The instruction card for this work filled several typewritten pages, and described in detail the order in which the operations should be done and the exact details of each man's work, with the number of each tool required, piece work prices, etc.

The whole scheme was much laughed at when it first went into use, but the trouble taken was fully justified, for the work was better done than ever before, and it cost only eleven dollars to completely overhaul a set of 300 H.P. boilers by this method, while the average cost of doing the same work on day work without an instruction card was sixty-two dollars.

Regarding the personal relations which should be maintained between employers and their men, the writer quotes the following paragraphs from a paper written in 1895. Additional experience has only served to confirm and strengthen these views; and although the greater part of this time, in his work of shop organization, has been devoted to the difficult and delicate task of inducing workmen to change their ways of doing things he has never been opposed by a strike.

"There has never been a strike by men working under this system, although it has been applied at the Midvale Steel Works for the past ten years; and the steel business has proved during this period the most fruitful field for labor organizations and strikes. And this notwithstanding the fact that the Midvale Company has never prevented its men from joining any labor organization. All of the best men in the company saw clearly that the success of a labor organization meant the lowering of their wages in order that the inferior men might earn more, and, of course, could not be persuaded to join.

"I attribute a great part of this success in avoiding strikes to the high wages which the best men were able to earn with the differential rates, and to the pleasant feeling fostered by this system; but this is by no means the whole cause. It has for years been the policy of that company to stimulate the personal ambition of every man in their employ by promoting them either in wages or position whenever they deserved it and the opportunity came.

"A careful record has been kept of each man's good points as well as his shortcomings, and one of the principal duties of each foreman was to make this careful study of his men so that substantial justice could be done to each. When men throughout an establishment are paid varying rates of day-work wages according to their individual worth, some being above and some below the average, it cannot be for the interest of those receiving high pay to join a union with the cheap men.

"No system of management, however good, should be applied in a wooden way. The proper personal relations should always be maintained between the employers and men; and even the prejudices of the workmen should be considered in dealing with them.

"The employer who goes through his works with kid gloves on, and is never known to dirty his hands or clothes, and who either talks to his men in a condescending or patronizing way, or else not at all, has no chance whatever of ascertaining their real thoughts or feelings.

"Above all is it desirable that men should be talked to on their own level by those who are over them. Each man should be encouraged to discuss any trouble which he may have, either in the works or outside, with those over him. Men would far rather even be blamed by their bosses, especially if the 'tearing out' has a touch of human nature and feeling in it, than to be passed by day after day without a word, and with no more notice than if they were part of the machinery.

"The opportunity which each man should have of airing his mind freely, and having it out with his employers, is a safety-valve; and if the superintendents are reasonable men, and listen to and treat with respect what their men have to say, there is absolutely no reason for labor unions and strikes.

"It is not the large charities (however generous they may be) that are needed or appreciated by workmen so much as small acts of personal kindness and sympathy, which establish a bond of friendly feeling between them and their employers.

"The moral effect of this system on the men is marked. The feeling that substantial justice is being done them renders them on the whole much more manly, straightforward, and truthful. They work more cheerfully, and are more obliging to one another and their employers. They are not soured, as under the old system, by brooding over the injustice done them; and their spare minutes are not spent to the same extent in criticizing their employers."

The writer has a profound respect for the working men of this country. He is proud to say that he has as many firm friends among them as among his other friends who were born in a different class, and he believes that quite as many men of fine character and ability are to be found among the former as in the latter. Being himself a college educated man, and having filled the various positions of foreman, master mechanic, chief draftsman, chief engineer, general superintendent, general manager, auditor, and head of the sales department, on the one hand, and on the other hand having been for several years a workman, as apprentice, laborer, machinist, and gang boss, his sympathies are equally divided between the two classes.

He is firmly convinced that the best interests of workmen and their employers are the same; so that in his criticism of labor unions he feels that he is advocating the interests of both sides. The following paragraphs on this subject are quoted from the paper written in 1895 and above referred to:

"The author is far from taking the view held by many manufacturers that labor unions are an almost unmitigated detriment to those who join them, as well as to employers and the general public.

"The labor unions—particularly the trades unions of England— have rendered a great service, not only to their members, but to the world, in shortening the hours of labor and in modifying the hardships and improving the conditions of wage workers.

"In the writer's judgment the system of treating with labor unions would seem to occupy a middle position among the various methods of adjusting the relations between employers and men.

"When employers herd their men together in classes, pay all of each class the same wages, and offer none of them any inducements to work harder or do better than the average, the only remedy for the men lies in combination; and frequently the only possible answer to encroachments on the part of their employers is a strike.

"This state of affairs is far from satisfactory to either employers or men, and the writer believes the system of regulating the wages and conditions of employment of whole classes of men by conference and agreement between the leaders of unions and manufacturers to be vastly inferior, both in its moral effect on the men and on the material interests of both parties, to the plan of stimulating each workman's ambition by paying him according to his individual worth, and without limiting him to the rate of work or pay of the average of his class."

The amount of work which a man should do in a day, what constitutes proper pay for this work, and the maximum number of hours per day which a man should work, together form the most important elements which are discussed between workmen and their employers. The writer has attempted to show that these matters can be much better determined by the expert time student than by either the union or a board of directors, and he firmly believes that in the future scientific time study will establish standards which will be accepted as fair by both sides.

There is no reason why labor unions should not be so constituted as to be a great help both to employers and men. Unfortunately, as they now exist they are in many, if not most, cases a hindrance to the prosperity of both.

The chief reasons for this would seem to be a failure on the part of the workmen to understand the broad principles which affect their best interests as well as those of their employers. It is undoubtedly true, however, that employers as a whole are not much better informed nor more interested in this matter than their workmen.

One of the unfortunate features of labor unions as they now exist is that the members look upon the dues which they pay to the union, and the time that they devote to it, as an investment which should bring them an annual return, and they feel that unless they succeed in getting either an increase in wages or shorter hours every year or so, the money which they pay into the union is wasted. The leaders of the unions realize this and, particularly if they are paid for their services, are apt to spend considerable of their time scaring up grievances whether they exist or not This naturally fosters antagonism instead of friendship between the two sides. There are, of course, marked exceptions to this rule; that of the Brotherhood of Locomotive Engineers being perhaps the most prominent.

The most serious of the delusions and fallacies under which workmen, and particularly those in many of the unions, are suffering is that it is for their interest to limit the amount of work which a man should do in a day.

There is no question that the greater the daily output of the average individual in a trade the greater will be the average wages earned in the trade, and that in the long run turning out a large amount of work each day will give them higher wages, steadier and more work, instead of throwing them out of work. The worst thing that a labor union can do for its members in the long run is to limit the amount of work which they allow each workman to do in a day. If their employers are in a competitive business, sooner or later those competitors whose workmen do not limit the output will take the trade away from them, and they will be thrown out of work. And in the meantime the small day's work which they have accustomed themselves to do demoralizes them, and instead of developing as men do when they use their strength and faculties to the utmost, and as men should do from year to year, they grow lazy, spend much of their time pitying themselves, and are less able to compete with other men. Forbidding their members to do more than a given amount of work in a day has been the greatest mistake made by the English trades unions. The whole of that country is suffering more or less from this error now. Their workmen are for this reason receiving lower wages than they might get, and in many cases the men, under the influence of this idea, have grown so slow that they would find it difficult to do a good day's work even if public opinion encouraged them in it.

In forcing their members to work slowly they use certain cant phrases which sound most plausible until their real meaning is analyzed. They continually use the expression, "Workmen should not be asked to do more than a fair day's work," which sounds right and just until we come to see how it is applied. The absurdity of its usual application would be apparent if we were to apply it to animals. Suppose a contractor had in his stable a miscellaneous collection of draft animals, including small donkeys, ponies, light horses, carriage horses and fine dray horses, and a law were to be made that no animal in the stable should be allowed to do more than "a fair day's work" for a donkey. The injustice of such a law would be apparent to every one. The trades unions, almost without an exception, admit all of those in the trade to membership—providing they pay their dues. And the difference between the first-class men and the poor ones is quite as great as that between fine dray horses and donkeys. In the case of horses this difference is well known to every one; with men, however, it is not at all generally recognized. When a labor union, under the cloak of the expression "a fair day's work," refuses to allow a first-class man to do any more work than a slow or inferior workman can do, its action is quite as absurd as limiting the work of a fine dray horse to that of a donkey would be.

Promotion, high wages, and, in some cases, shorter hours of work are the legitimate ambitions of a workman, but any scheme which curtails the output should be recognized as a device for lowering wages in the long run.

Any limit to the maximum wages which men are allowed to earn in a trade is equally injurious to their best interests. The "minimum wage" is the least harmful of the rules which are generally adopted by trades unions, though it frequently works an injustice to the better workmen. For example, the writer has

131

been used to having his machinists earn all the way from $1.50 to seven and eight dollars per day, according to the individual worth of the men. Supposing a rule were made that no machinist should be paid less than $2.50 per day. It is evident that if an employer were forced to pay $2.50 per day to men who were only worth $1.50 or $1.75, in order to compete he would be obliged to lower the wages of those who in the past were getting more than $2.50, thus pulling down the better workers in order to raise up the poorer men. Men are not born equal, and any attempt to make them so is contrary to nature's laws and will fail.

Some of the labor unions have succeeded in persuading the people in parts of this country that there is something sacred in the cause of union labor and that, in the interest of this cause, the union should receive moral support whether it is right in any particular case or not.

Union labor is sacred just so long as its acts are fair and good, and it is damnable just as soon as its acts are bad. Its rights are precisely those of nonunion labor, neither greater nor less. The boycott, the use of force or intimidation, and the oppression of non-union workmen by labor unions are damnable; these acts of tyranny are thoroughly un-American and will not be tolerated by the American people.

One of the most interesting and difficult problems connected with the art of management is how to persuade union men to do a full day's work if the union does not wish them to do it. I am glad of the opportunity of saying what I think on the matter, and of explaining somewhat in detail just how I should expect, in fact, how I have time after time induced union men to do a large day's work, quite as large as other men do.

In dealing with union men certain general principles should never be lost sight of. These principles are the proper ones to apply to all men, but in dealing with union men their application becomes all the more imperative.

132

First. One should be sure, beyond the smallest doubt, that what is demanded of the men is entirely just and can surely be accomplished. This certainty can only be reached by a minute and thorough time study.

Second. Exact and detailed directions should be given to the workman telling him, not in a general way but specifying in every small particular, just what he is to do and how he is to do it.

Third. It is of the utmost importance in starting to make a change that the energies of the management should be centered upon one single workman, and that no further attempt at improvement should be made until entire success has been secured in this case. Judgment should be used in selecting for a start work of such a character that the most clear cut and definite directions can be given regarding it, so that failure to carry out these directions will constitute direct disobedience of a single, straightforward order.

Fourth. In case the workman fails to carry out the order the management should be prepared to demonstrate that the work called for can be done by having some one connected with the management actually do it in the time called for.

The mistake which is usually made in dealing with union men, lies in giving an order which affects a number of workmen at the same time and in laying stress upon the increase in the output which is demanded instead of emphasizing one by one the details which the workman is to carry out in order to attain the desired result. In the first case a clear issue is raised: say that the man must turn out fifty per cent more pieces than he has in the past, and therefore it will be assumed by most people that he must work fifty per cent harder. In this issue the union is more than likely to have the sympathy of the general public, and they can logically take it up and fight upon it. If, however, the workman is given a series of plain, simple, and reasonable orders, and is offered a premium for carrying them out, the union will have a much more difficult task in defending the man who disobeys them. To illustrate: If we take the case of a complicated piece of machine work which is being done on a lathe or other machine tool, and the workman is called upon (under the old type of management) to increase his output by twenty-five or fifty per cent there is opened a field of argument in which the assertion of the man, backed by the union, that the task is impossible or too hard, will have quite as much weight as that of the management. If, however, the management begins by analyzing in detail just how each section of the work should be done and then writes out complete instructions specifying the tools to be used in succession, the cone step on which the driving belt is to run, the depth of cut and the feed to be used, the exact manner in which the work is to be set in the machine, etc., and if before starting to make any change they have trained in as functional foremen several men who are particularly expert and well informed in their specialties, as, for instance, a speed boss, gang boss, and inspector; if you then place for example a speed boss alongside of that workman, with an instruction card clearly written out, stating what both the speed boss and the man whom he is instructing are to do, and that card says you are to use such and such a tool, put your driving belt on this cone, and use this feed on your machine, and if you do so you will get out the work in such and such a time, I can hardly conceive of a case in which a union could prevent the boss from ordering the man to put his driving belt just where he said and using just the feed that he said, and in doing that the workman can hardly fail to get the work out on time. No union would dare to say to the management of a works, you shall not run the machine with the belt on this or that cone step. They do not come down specifically in that way; they say, "You shall not work so fast," but they do not say, "You shall not use such and such a tool, or run with such a feed or at such a speed." However much they might like to do it, they do not dare to interfere specifically in this way. Now, when your single man under the supervision of a speed boss, gang boss, etc., runs day after day at the given speed and feed, and gets work out in the time that the instruction card calls for, and when a premium is kept for him in the office for having done the work in the required time, you begin to have a moral suasion on that workman which is very powerful. At first he won't take the premium if it is contrary to the laws of his union, but as time goes on and it piles up and amounts to a big item, he will be apt to step into the office and ask for his premium, and before long your man will be a thorough convert to the new system. Now, after one man has been persuaded, by means of the four functional foremen, etc., that he will earn more money under the new system than under the laws of the union, you can then take the next man, and so convert one after another right through your shop, and as time goes on public opinion will swing around more and more rapidly your way.

I have a profound respect for the workmen of the United States; they are in the main sensible men—not all of them, of course, but they are just as sensible as are those on the side of the management There are some fools among them; so there are among the men who manage industrial plants. They are in many respects misguided men, and they require a great deal of information that they have not got. So do most managers.

All that most workmen need to make them do what is right is a series of proper object lessons. When they are convinced that a system is offered them which will yield them larger returns than the union provides for, they will promptly acquiesce. The necessary object lessons can best be given by centering the efforts of the management upon one spot. The mistake that ninety-nine men out of a hundred make is that they have attempted to influence a large body of men at once instead of taking one man at a time.

Another important factor is the question of time. If any one expects large results in six months or a year in a very large works he is looking for the impossible. If any one expects to

135

convert union men to a higher rate of production, coupled with high wages, in six months or a year, he is expecting next to an impossibility. But if he is patient enough to wait for two or three years, he can go among almost any set of workmen in the country and get results.

Some method of disciplining the men is unfortunately a necessary element of all systems of management. It is important that a consistent, carefully considered plan should be adopted for this as for all other details of the art. No system of discipline is at all complete which is not sufficiently broad to cover the great variety in the character and disposition of the various men to be found in a shop.

There is a large class of men who require really no discipline in the ordinary acceptance of the term; men who are so sensitive, conscientious and desirous of doing just what is right that a suggestion, a few words of explanation, or at most a brotherly admonition is all that they require. In all cases, therefore, one should begin with every new man by talking to him in the most friendly way, and this should be repeated several times over until it is evident that mild treatment does not produce the desired effect.

Certain men are both thick-skinned and coarse-grained, and these individuals are apt to mistake a mild manner and a kindly way of saying things for timidity or weakness. With such men the severity both of words and manner should be gradually increased until either the desired result has been attained or the possibilities of the English language have been exhausted.

Up to this point all systems of discipline should be alike. There will be found in all shops, however, a certain number of men with whom talk, either mild or severe, will have little or no effect, unless it produces the conviction that something more tangible and disagreeable will come next. The question is what this something shall be.

136

Discharging the men is, of course, effective as far as that individual is concerned, and this is in all cases the last step; but it is desirable to have several remedies between talking and discharging more severe than the one and less drastic than the other.

Usually one or more of the following expedients are adopted for this purpose:

First. Lowering the man's wages.

Second. Laying him off for a longer or shorter period of time.

Third. Fining him.

Fourth. Giving him a series of "bad marks," and when these sum up to more than a given number per week or month, applying one or the other of the first three remedies.

The general objections to the first and second expedients is that for a large number of offenses they are too severe, so that the disciplinarian hesitates to apply them. The men find this out, and some of them will take advantage of this and keep much of the time close to the limit. In laying a man off, also, the employer is apt to suffer as much in many cases as the man, through having machinery lying idle or work delayed. The fourth remedy is also objectionable because some men will deliberately take close to their maximum of "bad marks."

In the writer's experience, the fining system, if justly and properly applied, is more effective and much to be preferred to either of the others. He has applied this system of discipline in various works with uniform success over a long period of years, and so far as he knows, none of those who have tried it under his directions have abandoned it.

The success of the fining system depends upon two elements:

137

First. The impartiality, good judgment and justice with which it is applied.

Second. Every cent of the fines imposed should in some form be returned to the workmen. If any part of the fines is retained by the company, it is next to impossible to keep the workmen from believing that at least a part of the motive in fining them is to make money out of them; and this thought works so much harm as to more than overbalance the good effects of the system. If, however, all of the fines are in some way promptly returned to the men, they recognize it as purely a system of discipline, and it is so direct, effective and uniformly just that the best men soon appreciate its value and approve of it quite as much as the company.

In many cases the writer has first formed a mutual beneficial association among the employees, to which all of the men as well as the company contribute. An accident insurance association is much safer and less liable to be abused than a general sickness or life insurance association; so that, when practicable, an association of this sort should be formed and managed by the men. All of the fines can then be turned over each week to this association and so find their way directly back to the men. Like all other elements, the fining system should not be plunged into head first. It should be worked up to gradually and with judgment, choosing at first only the most flagrant cases for fining and those offenses which affect the welfare of some of the other workmen. It will not be properly and most effectively applied until small offenses as well as great receive their appropriate fine. The writer has fined men from one cent to as high as sixty dollars per fine. It is most important that the fines should be applied absolutely impartially to all employees, high and low. The writer has invariably fined himself just as he would the men under him for all offenses committed.

The fine is best applied in the form of a request to contribute a certain amount to the mutual beneficial association, with the

138

understanding that unless this request is complied with the man will be discharged.

In certain cases the fining system may not produce the desired result, so that coupled with it as an additional means of disciplining the men should be the first and second expedients of "lowering wages" and "laying the men off for a longer or shorter time"

The writer does not at all depreciate the value of the many semi-philanthropic and paternal aids and improvements, such as comfortable lavatories, eating rooms, lecture halls, and free lectures, night schools, kindergartens, baseball and athletic grounds, village improvement societies, and mutual beneficial associations, unless done for advertising purposes. This kind of so-called welfare work all tends to improve and elevate the workmen and make life better worth living. Viewed from the managers' standpoint they are valuable aids in making more intelligent and better workmen, and in promoting a kindly feeling among the men for their employers. They are, however, of distinctly secondary importance, and should never be allowed to engross the attention of the superintendent to the detriment of the more important and fundamental elements of management. They should come in all establishments, but they should come only after the great problem of work and wages has been permanently settled to the satisfaction of both parties. The solution of this problem will take more than the entire time of the management in the average case for several years.

Mr. Patterson, of the National Cash Register Company, of Dayton, Ohio, has presented to the world a grand object lesson of the combination of many philanthropic schemes with, in many respects, a practical and efficient management. He stands out a pioneer in this work and an example of a kindhearted and truly successful man. Yet I feel that the recent strike in his works demonstrates all the more forcibly my contention that the establishment of the semi-philanthropic schemes should follow instead of preceding the solution of the wages question; unless, as is very rarely the case, there are brains, energy and money enough available in a company to establish both elements at the same time.

Unfortunately there is no school of management. There is no single establishment where a relatively large part of the details of management can be seen, which represent the best of their kinds. The finest developments are for the most part isolated, and in many cases almost buried with the mass of rubbish which surrounds them.

Among the many improvements for which the originators will probably never receive the credit which they deserve the following may be mentioned.

The remarkable system for analyzing all of the work upon new machines as the drawings arrived from the drafting-room and of directing the movement and grouping of the various parts as they progressed through the shop, which was developed and used for several years by Mr. Wm. II. Thorne, of Wm. Sellers & Co., of Philadelphia, while the company was under the general management of Mr. J. Sellers Bancroft. Unfortunately the full benefit of this method was never realized owing to the lack of the other functional elements which should have accompanied it.

And then the employment bureau which forms such an important element of the Western Electric Company in Chicago; the complete and effective system for managing the messenger boys introduced by Mr. Almon Emrie while superintendent of the Ingersoll Sargent Drill Company, of Easton, Pa.; the mnemonic system of order numbers invented by Mr. Oberlin Smith and amplified by Mr. Henry R. Towne, of The Yale & Towne Company, of Stamford, Conn.; and the system of inspection introduced by Mr. Chas. D. Rogers in the works of the American Screw Company, at Providence, R. I. and the many good points in the apprentice system developed by Mr. Vauclain, of the Baldwin Locomotive Works, of Philadelphia.

The card system of shop returns invented and introduced as a complete system by Captain Henry Metcalfe, U. S. A., in the government shops of the Frankford Arsenal represents another such distinct advance in the art of management. The writer appreciates the difficulty of this undertaking as he was at the same time engaged in the slow evolution of a similar system in the Midvale Steel Works, which, however, was the result of a gradual development instead of a complete, well thought out invention as was that of Captain Metcalfe.

The writer is indebted to most of these gentlemen and to many others, but most of all to the Midvale Steel Company, for elements of the system which he has described. The rapid and successful application of the general principles involved in any system will depend largely upon the adoption of those details which have been found in actual service to be most useful. There are many such elements which the writer feels should be described in minute detail. It would, however, be improper to burden this record with matters of such comparatively small importance.